Monika Römer   Oliver Brachat

Christmas Cookies

Dozens of Classic Yuletide Treats for the Whole Family

Skyhorse Publishing

English Copyright © 2015 by Skyhorse Publishing, Inc.

Original Edition © 2012 Hölker Verlag im Coppenrath Verlag GmbH & Co. KG, Münster, Germany.

Original Title: *Unsere Weihnachtsbäckerei* (ISBN 978-3-88117-868-6). All rights reserved.

Skyhorse Publishing books may be purchased in bulk at special discounts for sales promotion, corporate gifts, fund-raising, or educational purposes. Special editions can also be created to specifications. For details, contact the Special Sales Department, Skyhorse Publishing, 307 West 36th Street, 11th Floor, New York, NY 10018 or info@skyhorsepublishing.com.

Skyhorse® and Skyhorse Publishing® are registered trademarks of Skyhorse Publishing, Inc.®, a Delaware corporation.

Visit our website at www.skyhorsepublishing.com.

10 9 8 7 6 5 4 3 2 1

Library of Congress Cataloging-in-Publication Data is available on file.

Cover design by Georgia Morrissey

Cover photography by Oliver Brachat

Print ISBN: 978-1-63450-365-5
Ebook ISBN: 978-1-5107-0117-5

Printed in China

Contents

The following symbols will be used in this book:

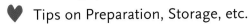 Tips on Preparation, Storage, etc.

Tips on Decorating and Packaging

Christmas Bakery

Welcome to the Christmas Bakery

Christmas and baking cookies simply go hand in hand. Surely the anticipation of the irresistible fragrances wafting out of the local bakery and the scents from your own oven cause you to recall your childhood. There are tins to fill with homemade treats, and family and friends to spoil with those delicious creations. But more than anything else, you achieve an exquisite taste experience when you bake Christmas cookies with high-quality ingredients.

The Details Are Important

For Christmas baking, use exclusively fresh, natural, high-quality ingredients. This is especially important for butter, eggs, almonds, nuts, pistachios, and the typical Christmas spices. Try not to use any synthetic ingredients; use only fresh zest from organic lemons and oranges and unsulphured raisins, currants, and other dried fruits. If you work with whole-grain flour, it should be freshly ground, if possible.

The recipes in this book are very easy if you pay attention to all the details in the instructions: measure or weigh the ingredients precisely and adhere to the specifications exactly—particularly cooling times, baking temperatures, and baking times—to make sure that everything goes smoothly. If you have not baked much using your own oven, it is worth it to look over the instructions for use and perhaps bake a few test batches. Make yourself a note for the next time if you have an experience different from the ones described in this book.

Marzipan

Marzipan is not uncommon in Christmas baking. Even though you can make it yourself, industrially produced marzipan paste is widely available and of such good quality that you do not need to make this effort.

Christmas Bakery

Tempered Couverture or Cake Glaze?

Couverture chocolate is often seen in sweet shops and in patisserie-produced chocolate. It is made from cocoa paste, cocoa butter, and sugar and is thinner than melted bars of chocolate. The quality, like that of any chocolate, is dependent on the percentage of high-quality cocoa beans and on the content of the cocoa mass in ratio with the sugar content. The higher the quality of the beans and the higher the cocoa mass ratio, the more bitter the taste of the chocolate.

The temperature of the couverture is crucial to the silky sheen of a chocolate glaze both before and during its processing. Because of this, the couverture must, with the help of a special thermometer (which is sold in specialty baking stores at affordable prices), be carefully tempered.

The so-called injection method works best. First, a large piece of the required couverture chocolate is coarsely chopped and slowly melted (don't heat higher than 105°F [40°C] or it will separate). Then add finely grated couverture chocolate, little by little, until the mixture thickens, the flakes of chocolate slowly dissolve, and the chocolate has a temperature of 86–91°F (30–33°C). To test whether it is the right temperature, briefly insert a palette knife and then remove the knife from the chocolate. The knife must come out shiny and smooth and not have any streaks.

Anyone who does not want to make this effort should make a prepackaged chocolate glaze instead, as a couverture that has not been heated to the right temperature quickly turns an unattractive gray color. A cake glaze has a nice shine, but it does not compare to a good couverture chocolate.

Schedule and Storage

At the beginning of the Advent season, you should make a plan for when you want to do your baking. Ideally, you should make the baked goods that taste better with time first. These include gingerbread, honey cake, Springerle cookies, and macaroons. On the other hand, baked goods like butter cookies can also be stored, and even frozen, but they taste best fresh. To store baked goods, it is best to use clean, odorless, and airtight tins or food storage boxes. It is important that each different type of cake or cookie is packed in a separate container so they retain their original flavors.

Editor's Note: German baking soda is not the same as American baking soda. You can often substitute double-acting baking powder for single-acting, slow-rising baking powder in German recipes. If you would like to approximate German baking powder you can mix readily-available cream of tartar with baking soda in a 2:1 ratio. You may order German baking soda online or at specialty stores.

Baking with Children

Baking with children during Christmastime is a joyful experience. It is no problem if the little Christmas bakers require help from an adult or an older sibling. Older children can bake a few recipes from this book almost entirely alone. However, every child should receive help from an adult when inserting and removing baking sheets from the oven.

✳ In each recipe for kids, you will find one, two, or three stars. These will indicate which ones are easy *, somewhat difficult **, and complex ***.

Professional tips for baking beginners

1 Very important: always measure exactly according to what is written in the recipe!

2 Unless otherwise indicated, all ingredients should be at room temperature.

3 If baking powder is an ingredient in the recipe, always mix the baking powder with the flour first, before it is kneaded into a dough with the rest of the ingredients!

4 Dough can be kneaded by hand or with a hand mixer.

5 When rolling out dough, always sprinkle some flour onto the rolling pin and the work surface.

6 Line baking sheets with parchment paper so that cookies can be easily removed.

7 Unless otherwise stated, baked goods should be baked on the middle rack.

8 Two oven mitts should be kept ready for when it is time to remove the cookies from the oven.

9 Once baked goods come out of the oven, let them cool completely and then store in separate airtight containers, according to type, until it is time for them to be consumed.

10 And one more thing that is also quite important: after baking, all used kitchen appliances and dishes should be washed and the kitchen cleaned up!

Christmas Bakery

Practical Kitchen Appliances

Help the little bakers get familiar with the kitchen appliances they will need during Christmas baking. The main appliances used are pictured here, but do not worry— for some of the baked goods in this book, very little is needed, such as 2 teaspoons or a few cookie cutters.

1 Hand Mixer

2 Bowl

3 Baking Tray

4 Rubber Scrapers

5 Cookie Cutters

6 Liter Measuring Cup

7 Mincer

8 Rolling Pin

9 Wooden Spoon

10 Cooling Rack

11 Paper Muffin/Cupcake Liners

12 Small Sieve

13 Cookie Press

14 Citrus Juicer

15 Parchment Paper

16 Attachments for the Cookie Press

Christmas Bakery

Colorful Cookies

German Advent and Christmas culture is world famous due to many diverse regional traditions, especially those relating to baked goods. Let these classic Christmas cookies inspire you. When the subtle scents of fruit-filled biscuits, wonderfully tender vanilla crescents, sweet marzipan pastries, or crispy hazelnut cookies waft through the house, you can't help but be in a festive mood!

Butter Cookie Christmas Trees

MAKES 2 TRAYS
For the dough: 3 cups + 2 tsp (380 g) flour, 1 pinch salt, 1 cup (120 g) powdered sugar, 1 cup + 1½ tbsp (250 g) cold butter, 2 egg yolks
For the icing: ²/₃ cup + 2 tbsp + 2 tsp (100 g) powdered sugar, 1–2 tbsp lemon juice
Additional: extra flour to coat parchment paper

On a countertop, mix flour, salt, and sugar. Cut the butter into small pieces and mix it into the flour mixture until crumbly. Add in the egg yolks and knead everything into a smooth dough. Form into balls, wrap them in plastic wrap, and let them rest for 30 minutes in the refrigerator.

Preheat the oven to 355°F (180°C), unless you have a convection oven, in which case preheat to 320°F (160°C), or a gas oven, in which case preheat to level 3. Roll out the dough approximately ¹/₁₀ in. (3 mm) thick, on a lightly floured countertop, and cut out stars or snowflakes in three different sizes. Place the cookies onto the baking sheets, which should be lined with parchment paper. Bake one tray at a time in the preheated oven (middle rack) for approximately 10 minutes each, until the cookies are light brown. Remove them from the parchment paper while they are still hot and let them cool on a cooling rack. Make a glaze by mixing sifted powdered sugar and lemon juice.

Make a conical piping bag out of parchment paper, fill it with the glaze, and cut a small hole at the tip of the bag. Squeeze the icing onto the cookies diagonally, in fine lines, and place onto a cooling rack to let the icing harden a bit. Then place the butter cookies on top of each other to form little Christmas trees (see photo), starting with the largest cookies, and then using those that are smaller, in a consecutive order.

 It goes without saying that you can create many individual cookies from this dough, using any Christmas-themed cookie cutters you'd like. Bake as written above and drizzle with either couverture heated to the right temperature (see page 10–11) or a chocolate glaze.

 You can display an especially beautiful butter cookie Christmas tree on a cake plate with a glass lid.

Colorful Cookies

Linzer Cookies

MAKES 2 TRAYS

For the dough: 3 cups + 2 tsp (380 g) flour, 1 pinch salt, 1 cup (120 g) powdered sugar, 1 cup + 1½ tbsp (250 g) cold butter, 2 egg yolks
For decorating: 9 oz (250 g) red or yellow jam, 1 tbsp rum or water
Additional: assorted cookie cutters (wavy-edged circles, flowers, stars), powdered sugar for garnishing, plastic wrap

On a countertop, mix flour, salt, and powdered sugar. Cut the butter into small pieces and rub into the flour mixture until crumbly. Add the egg yolks and knead everything together into a smooth dough. Form into balls, wrap them in plastic wrap, and let them rest for 30 minutes in the refrigerator.

Preheat the oven to 355°F (180°C), unless you have a convection oven, in which case preheat to 320°F (160°C), or a gas oven, in which case preheat to level 3. Roll out the dough 3 mm thick and cut out an even number of cookies using the wavy-edged circle, flower, or star cookie cutters. In half of the cookies, cut out a hole of any shape, $^2/_5$ in. (1 cm) in diameter. Place cookies on the baking sheets, which should be lined with parchment paper. Bake one tray at a time in the preheated oven (middle rack), each for approximately 10 minutes, until the cookies are light brown. During this time, heat the jam with rum or water.

Remove the cookies from the parchment paper while they are still hot. Place ½ tsp jam on the cookies without holes in them and place a cookie with a hole on top. Sprinkle with powdered sugar immediately.

♥ With certain cookie cutters, you can cut out each shape and its inner hole at the same time, which makes the work go faster.

Colorful Cookies

Black and White Cookies

MAKES 1 TRAY

For the dough: 2$^1/_3$ cups (290 g) flour, 1 tsp baking powder, 1 cup + 2 tsp (125 g) powdered sugar, 1 pinch salt, $^2/_3$ cup (150 g) cold butter, 1 egg yolk, 3 tsp cocoa powder
Additional: flour to knead in, milk to brush on top of the dough, plastic wrap

On a countertop, mix flour, baking powder, powdered sugar, and salt. Cut the butter into small pieces and add to the flour mixture until crumbly. Add the egg yolk and combine everything together into a smooth dough. Split the dough into two equal halves and knead the cocoa powder into one of them. Form each piece of dough into a ball, wrap in plastic wrap, and let sit in the refrigerator for 2 hours.

Roll out both pieces of dough on a floured work surface to be exactly $^2/_5$ in. (1 cm) thick squares. Then cut into $^2/_5$ in. (1 cm) wide strips. Lay a light strip, a dark strip, and again a light strip next to each other, brush the adjacent edges with a little bit of milk, and join together. Repeat this process again. Wrap the square pieces of dough in plastic wrap and place in the freezer for 10 minutes so they can be cut more easily.

Preheat the oven to 355°F (180°C), unless you have a convection oven, in which case preheat to 320°F (160°C), or a gas oven, in which case preheat to level 3. Line a baking sheet with parchment paper. Cut the pieces of dough into $^1/_{10}$ in. (3 mm) thick slices with a sharp knife and lay them next to each other on the baking sheet. Bake in preheated oven (middle rack) for 12 minutes until lightly colored. Remove from the oven and let cool on a wire rack.

Colorful Cookies

Vanilla Crescents

MAKES 1 TRAY

For the dough: 2¼ cups (280 g) wheat flour, ½ cup + 1¼ tsp (50 g) ground almonds, ½ cup (50 g) ground hazelnuts, $^1/_3$ cup (70 g) sugar, 1 pinch salt, ¾ cup + 3 tbsp (210 g) cold butter
Additional: flour to knead in, ½ cup + $^1/_3$ cup (100 g) powdered sugar, and ½ cup (100 g) granulated sugar to roll the cookies in, 1 whole vanilla pod

For the dough, pour flour, almonds, hazelnuts, sugar, and salt out onto the countertop. Cut the butter into small pieces, rub it into the rest of the ingredients until crumbly, and knead into a smooth dough. Shape it into a cylindrical roll about 2 in. (5 cm) thick, wrap it in plastic wrap, and let rest for 2 hours in the refrigerator.

Preheat the oven to 355°F (180°C), unless you have a convection oven, in which case preheat to 320°F (160°C), or a gas oven, in which case preheat to level 3. Cut the roll of dough into finger-thick slices and, with floured hands, form into tapered crescents. Place on a baking sheet lined with parchment paper. Bake in preheated oven (middle rack) for 12 minutes until lightly colored.

Meanwhile, mix the powdered sugar with the granulated sugar to make the coating for the cookies. Cut open the vanilla pod, scrape out the pulp, and mix it in with the sugar mixture. Remove the vanilla crescents from the oven, and while they are still hot, use two forks to very carefully roll them in the vanilla sugar.

♥ Caution: When the vanilla crescents are still warm, they are very fragile.

♥ If you want to make your own reserves of vanilla sugar, place the scratched-out pulp from a vanilla bean in a jar (pint-sized [500 ml in volume], with a clip lock) with granulated sugar and let the mixture stand for approximately two weeks.

Colorful Cookies

Browned Butter Shortbread Cookies

MAKES 1 TRAY

For the dough: 1 cup + 1½ tbsp (250 g) butter, ½ vanilla pod, 1 cup (200 g) sugar, ½ tsp salt, 2¾ cup + 1 tbsp (350 g) wheat flour or spelt flour

Additional: parchment paper

Heat butter slowly in a small pot over low heat, stirring continuously, until it is slightly brown. Pour into a mixing bowl and let it harden. Slice open the vanilla pod, scrape out the pulp, and add to the browned butter. Add sugar and salt, as well, and beat the mixture using a hand mixer with a whisk attachment until creamy. Fold in the flour carefully.

Lay two pieces of parchment paper on a countertop. Cut the dough in half and place each half in the center of a piece of paper. With help of the parchment paper, form two identically shaped cylindrical rolls, approx. 1¾ in. (4½ cm) in diameter, and squeeze each of them firmly so they hold together. Keep covered in the refrigerator for 1 hour.

Preheat the oven to 355°F (180°C), unless you have a convection oven, in which case preheat to 320°F (160°C), or a gas oven, in which case preheat to level 3. Line a baking sheet with parchment paper. Take the rolls of dough out of the parchment paper, cut them into $^1/_8$ in. (4 mm) thick slices, and lay them on the cookie sheet. Place them in the preheated oven (on the middle rack) and bake 12 minutes until they are light brown.

Place the cookies, along with the paper, onto a countertop and let cool.

♥ Warning: The cookies are very breakable when they are still warm. If you use spelt flour, they will be even more fragile.

Colorful Cookies

Bear Claws (Madeleines)

MAKES 1 SHEET OF MADELEINES

For the dough: ½ cup + 1 tbsp (125 g) butter, 1 cup (125 g) flour, ½ cup + 2 tbsp (125 g) sugar, 3 eggs, 1 pinch salt, ½ cup + 2 tbsp (60 g) ground almonds (blanched), 1 tbsp orange blossom water (drug store or pharmacy), ½ tsp vanilla extract
Additional: pastry spatula, butter for the baking sheet, powdered sugar for sprinkling on top

Melt the butter, without browning it, and let it cool again. Sift the flour onto a countertop and add in the sugar. Make a hole in the mixture. Add the eggs into the hole and incorporate them into the mixture with a pastry spatula (not with your hands!). Then, little by little, add in the cooled butter, salt, ground almonds, orange blossom water, and vanilla extract. Quickly form the dough into a ball using your hands, wrap in plastic wrap, and let sit for 1 hour in the refrigerator.

Preheat the oven to 480°F (250°C), unless you have a convection oven, in which case preheat to 445°F (230°C), or a gas oven, in which case preheat to level 7–8. Grease a bear claw (aka madeleine) pan. Distribute the dough evenly, being sure to press it down into the molds. Place the pan into the preheated oven (on the middle rack) and bake for about 15 minutes, until the cookies are light brown. Take them out of the oven, remove them from the molds, and let cool on a wire rack. Sprinkle with powdered sugar before serving.

Colorful Cookies

Mini Sugar Pretzels

MAKES 1 TRAY

For the dough: 2 cups (250 g) flour, ²/₃ cup (150 g) cold butter, ½ cup (100 g) sugar, 1 pinch salt, 1 egg yolk, 1 tbsp cream, 1 tbsp lemon juice
For decorating: ¹/₃ cup + 4 tsp (50 g) powdered sugar, 1 tbsp rum, ¼ cup (50 g) coarse sugar
Additional: plastic wrap, parchment paper

Quickly knead flour with butter, sugar, salt, egg yolk, cream, and lemon juice into a smooth dough. Form into balls, wrap in plastic wrap, and let sit in the refrigerator for 1 hour.

Preheat the oven to 390°F (200°C), unless you have a convection oven, in which case preheat to 355°F (180°C), or a gas oven, in which case preheat to level 4. Form cylindrical rolls of dough, each about as thick as a pen, cut into approximately 12 in. (30 cm) long pieces, and shape into pretzels (see photo). Place the pretzels onto a baking sheet lined with parchment paper, and bake in preheated oven (middle rack) for about 15 minutes, until light brown.

Sift the powdered sugar, mix it into a thin glaze with rum and 1 tbsp water, and brush the slightly warm pretzels with it. Roll the pretzels in coarse sugar, making sure to submerge all sides, and let dry.

 After cooling, you can add Christmas ribbon to the pretzels and use them as decoration on a Christmas wreath or Christmas tree.

Colorful Cookies

Jam-Filled Biscuits (Angel Eyes)

For the dough: 1¹/₃ cup + 2 tbsp (180 g) flour, ¼ cup (25 g) fine breadcrumbs, ¼ cup (50 g) sugar, 1 tsp vanilla sugar, zest from ½ organic lemon, 1 egg, ¼ cup + 1 tbsp (70 g) soft butter, ¼ cup (60 g) clarified butter
For decorating: approx. 5¼ oz (150 g) currant or raspberry jelly
Additional: flour to knead in, plastic wrap, parchment paper, wooden spoon

Quickly knead flour, breadcrumbs, sugar, vanilla sugar, lemon zest, egg, butter, and lard into a smooth dough. Form into a ball, wrap in plastic wrap, and let rest in the refrigerator for 1 hour.

Preheat the oven to 355°F (180°C), unless you have a convection oven, in which case preheat to 320°F (160°C), or a gas oven, in which case preheat to level 3. Form the dough into balls just barely the size of walnuts, and place onto a baking sheet lined with parchment paper. Dip the handle of a wooden spoon in flour, and with that, make a little well in each ball. Fill the troughs with jam.

Place the jam-filled biscuits in preheated oven (middle rack) and bake until light brown, about 15 minutes. Remove from the oven, let cool, and place onto a wire rack.

Colorful Cookies

Mini Florentines

MAKES 2 TRAYS

For the dough: ¼ cup (60 g) butter, ⅓ cup (40 g) wheat flour or spelt flour, ½ cup (100 g) raw cane sugar, 1 pinch salt, ¼ cup (60 ml) cream, ¾ cup + 3 tbsp (100 g) sliced almonds
For the couverture chocolate: 7 oz (200 g) good-quality dark couverture chocolate or dark chocolate glaze
Additional: parchment paper

Mix butter, flour, sugar, salt, and cream in a bowl. Mix in the sliced almonds carefully. Preheat the oven to 355°F (180°C), unless you have a convection oven, in which case preheat to 320°F (160°C), or a gas oven, in which case preheat to level 3. Line baking sheets with parchment paper. Place dough on the baking sheets one teaspoon at a time, each mound a sufficient distance away from the others, as they tend to spread out during baking. Bake one tray after another in preheated oven (middle shelf) for 10–15 minutes, until the Florentines are an amber color. Remove the baking sheets from the oven. Take the Florentines, along with the parchment paper, off the baking sheets and let cool.

Temper the couverture (see pages 10–11) or melt the glaze according to the instructions on the package. Using two forks, dip the Florentines in either the couverture or chocolate glaze so that the underside of each one is coated. Place them on a cooling rack, chocolate-side up, and let harden.

 It is best to bake sample batches of florentines. If they're too hard, add a little bit of butter; but on the other hand, if the mixture is too soft, knead in a little bit of flour. You can also make the Florentines with candied cherries, candied lemon peel, candied orange peel, or sesame.

 Packaging: For this, you need a paper towel roll, wrapping paper, cellophane gift wrap, and ribbon. Cut a piece of the paper towel roll suitable for the number of cookies you are wrapping (see photo) and glue the wrapping paper of your choice to both sides. Cut out a large piece of cellophane and place it on the countertop. Then place the paper towel roll with wrapping paper glued onto it in the middle of the cellophane and stack the Florentines inside it. Carefully wrap the cellophane around the paper towel roll and seal from both the left and right sides with ribbon. If desired, you can also cut out a piece of wrapping paper to hang off the gift and attach it using a thin ribbon.

Colorful Cookies

Mini Nut Bars

MAKES 1 TRAY

For the dough: 1 cup + 3 tbsp (150 g) flour, ¼ cup + 2½ tsp (60 g) sugar, 2 tsp (8 g) vanilla sugar, 1 egg, ¼ cup (60 g) butter

For the couverture: ⅓ cup + 2 tbsp (100 g) butter, ½ cup (100 g) sugar, 2 tsp (8 g) vanilla sugar, 1 cup (100 g) ground hazelnuts, ½ cup + 1 tbsp (100 g) chopped hazelnuts, 7 oz (200 g) apricot jam

For decorating: 7 oz (200 g) good-quality dark couverture chocolate or dark chocolate glaze

Additional: flour to knead in, butter for the baking sheet, parchment paper, plastic wrap

For the dough, mix flour, sugar, and vanilla sugar in a bowl. Add in the egg and butter and knead into a smooth dough. Form into a ball, wrap in plastic wrap, and let rest for 30 minutes in the refrigerator.

In the meantime, for the topping, put butter, sugar, vanilla sugar, and 1 tbsp water in a pot and bring to a boil while stirring. Stir in the nuts, take the pot off the stove, and let cool slightly.

Preheat the oven to 355°F (180°C), unless you have a convection oven, in which case pre-heat to 320°F (160°C), or a gas oven, in which case preheat to level 3. Roll out the dough on a floured countertop and then lay it down on a greased baking sheet. Coat the dough with smooth, stirred apricot jam. Then spread the nut mixture evenly on top. Place in preheated oven (middle rack) and bake for 30 minutes, until golden brown. Remove the baking sheet from the oven and cut the dessert while it is still warm, first into squares, and then into triangles with edges that are approximately 3 in. (8 cm) long. Temper the couverture (see page 10–11), or melt the glaze according to the package instructions, dunk the corners of the nut bars in the couverture or glaze, and lay the cookies down on parchment paper to harden. After the chocolate is completely hard, store the nut bars in an airtight container.

Colorful Cookies

Hazelnut Biscuits

MAKES 1 TRAY

For the dough: ¼ cup + 1½ tbsp (80 g) soft butter, ²/₃ cup (200 g) liquid honey, 1 egg, 4 tbsp strong tea, ½ tsp cocoa powder, 1 tsp ground cinnamon, ½ tsp vanilla sugar, 1 pinch salt, ¹/₃ cup + 2 tbsp (80 g) finely chopped hazelnuts, 1½ cup + 5 tsp (200 g) whole-grain wheat flour, 1 tsp baking powder
For decorating: ¹/₃ cup (60 g) coarsely chopped hazelnuts, 1 egg white
Additional: flour to knead in, plastic wrap, parchment paper

Cream butter in a mixing bowl while adding in honey gradually using a hand mixer with a whisk attachment. Add in the egg, as well, and stir for about 1 minute. Then mix in tea, cocoa powder, cinnamon, vanilla sugar, salt, and finely chopped nuts. Sift the flour and baking powder and fold them in. On a floured countertop, knead the ingredients into a smooth dough and form into cylindrical rolls, 1–1½ in. (3–4 cm) in diameter. Wrap in plastic wrap and keep cold for several hours, or preferably, overnight.

Preheat the oven to 355°F (180°C), unless you have a convection oven, in which case preheat to 320°F (160°C), or a gas oven, in which case preheat to level 3. Line a baking sheet with parchment paper. Place the coarsely chopped hazelnuts on a plate. Whisk the egg white and brush the rolls of dough with it on all sides. Roll the pieces of dough in the chopped nuts until they are evenly covered. Then cut the dough with a sharp knife into approximately 3 mm thick slices and place them next to each other on the baking sheet.

Place in preheated oven (middle rack) and bake for about 15 minutes, until the biscuits are light brown. Take the baking sheets out of the oven, remove the biscuits along with the parchment paper, and let cool.

If you want to give the biscuits as gifts, they can be placed in a candy jar or in a canning jar with a lever closure. You can use jars of any size according to how many biscuits you want to give away.

Colorful Cookies

Filled Almond Cookies

MAKES 1 TRAY

For the dough: ¾ cup + 2 tbsp (200 g) soft butter, 1¼ cups (150 g) powdered sugar, 3 eggs, 1 pinch of salt, zest from 1 organic lemon, pulp from 1 vanilla bean, 1 cup + 1 tbsp (¼ l) cream, 2⅓ cups + 1 tbsp (300 g) flour, 1½ cups + 1 tbsp (150 g) ground almonds
To be sprinkled on top: ½ cup + 2 tsp (50 g) chopped almonds
For the filling: 1¾ oz (50 g) almond nougat (alternatively traditional nougat), ⅓ cup (75 g) butter
Additional: piping bag with a round tip, parchment paper

Preheat the oven to 390°F (200°C), unless you have a convection oven, in which case preheat to 355°F (180°C), or a gas oven, in which case preheat to level 4. Cream the butter with the powdered sugar and eggs. Add salt, lemon zest, and the scraped-out pulp from a vanilla pod. Add in the cream gradually. Mix the flour with the ground almonds and quickly fold in to the mixture.

Pour the batter into a piping bag with a round tip and squeeze circular cookies onto a baking sheet lined with parchment paper. Sprinkle with chopped almonds. Place into the preheated oven (middle rack) and bake for about 10 minutes, until light brown. Remove and let cool.

For the filling, stir the almond nougat with the butter in a bowl until creamy and then let melt in a double boiler. Assemble these treats by spreading nougat between two cookies to form sandwiches. Place on a wire rack and leave them there to harden.

♥ Let the almond cookies sit out overnight at room temperature before putting them in an airtight container to ensure the nougat filling has completely hardened.

Colorful Cookies

Anise Cookies

MAKES 2 TRAYS

For the dough: 1¼ cups (150 g) powdered sugar, 2 large eggs, 1 pinch salt, 2 tsp (8 oz) vanilla sugar, 1 cup + 3 tbsp (150 g) flour, 1 tsp ground star anise
Additional: icing bad with a round tip, butter and flour for the baking sheet

The dough can be prepared the day before, if necessary. Sift powdered sugar into a mixing bowl, and add in eggs, salt, and vanilla sugar. Place the bowl in a hot water bath and beat the ingredients using a hand mixer with the whisk attachment until the cream has reached a temperature of 105°F (40°C). Remove the bowl from the water bath and stir until the mixture is cold again. Then sift the flour onto the mixture and fold it in gently along with the star anise. Pour the mixture into the pastry bag and squeeze approximately quarter-sized circles onto the baking sheets, making sure not to place them too close together. Let harden at room temperature for 12 hours.

Then preheat the oven to 285°F (140°C), unless you have a convection oven, in which case preheat to 250°F (120°C), or a gas oven, in which case preheat to level 1. Grease the baking sheets and sprinkle with flour. Place the trays one at a time in the preheated oven (middle rack), and bake the cookies for 20–30 minutes. They are done when they brown slightly on the bottom but are still very light on top. Remove the anise cookies from the oven and let them cool on a wire rack. Store in an airtight container.

 You should prepare the anise cookies 2–3 weeks before they will be eaten so that they have plenty of time to become soft.

Colorful Cookies

Three Types of Macaroons

Basic recipe: 2 egg whites, 1 pinch salt, $^1/_3$ cup (75 g) raw cane sugar, $^1/_3$ cup + 2 tsp (75 g) sugar
For the coconut macaroons: 6 oz (170 g) shredded coconut
For the espresso macaroons: 1½ cups + 1 tbsp (150 g) ground almonds (blanched), 1 tbsp espresso or coffee powder (insoluble!), ¼ cup (20 g) sliced almonds
For the pistachio macaroons: 1½ cups (150 g) ground pistachios, 3 tbsp (20 g) coarsely chopped pistachios
Additional: parchment paper

Lightly beat the egg whites with the salt. Add the raw cane sugar and beat the mixture until stiff. While you are doing that, sprinkle the conventional white sugar into the bowl as well. Continue beating for 2 minutes. Depending on the flavor macaroons you are making, carefully fold in 5¼ oz (150 g) grated coconut, ground almonds, coffee powder, or ground pistachios.

Preheat the oven to 300°F (150°C), unless you have a convection oven, in which case preheat to 265°F (130°C), or a gas oven, in which case preheat to level 1. Line a baking sheet with parchment paper. Then, using 2 teaspoons, place little heaps of dough on the parchment paper and sprinkle with the remaining grated coconut, sliced almonds, or coarsely chopped pistachios, depending on which flavor macaroons you are making. Place the macaroons in the preheated oven (middle rack) and bake 12–15 minutes, until lightly colored.

 Box with four sections: Glue decorative paper onto a rectangular or square box, if desired (see instructions, page 74). To make two pieces of cardboard that will fit inside the box perfectly, cut the pieces according to the height and width of the inside of the box. On both pieces of cardboard, draw a vertical line down the center and mark the exact center point. Make a slit on each piece of cardboard, cutting along the line from one side and stopping once you reach the center point. Put the two pieces of cardboard together to form a cross and place the divider in the box. You can also cut tissue paper to size and place it in each section, if desired.

Colorful Cookies

 Marzipan Cookies

MAKES 1 TRAY
For the dough: 8¾ oz (250 g) marzipan paste, 2 small egg whites, 1 tsp lemon juice, 1 level tbsp flour, ½ cup + 2 tbsp (75 g) powdered sugar, 1 tsp rosewater
For decorating: 50 almonds (blanched)
Additional: parchment paper

Knead the marzipan, 1 egg white, lemon juice, flour, and powdered sugar with your hands. Make 30 cherry-sized balls out of the mixture. Cut the almonds in half. Place 3 almond halves, equally spaced from each other, upright on the sides of each ball (see photo). Press the almonds into the dough.

Preheat the oven to 285°F (140°C), unless you have a convection oven, in which case preheat to 250°F (120°C), or a gas oven, in which case preheat to level 1. Place the balls on a baking sheet lined with parchment paper. Mix the second egg white with the rosewater and brush the cookies with it. Bake in the preheated oven (middle rack) for about 40 minutes, until golden brown.

 Decorative round box: Packaged in a specially designed box, marzipan cookies can be an especially nice gift. You'll need a round box (if you don't already have one at home, you can find one in a craft store), a high-quality, stable wrapping paper of your choice, and self-adhesive tape (also found in craft stores). Trace the bottom of the box and then the side of the box on the proof-paper of the self-adhesive tape. Cut it out, leaving ²/₅ in. (1 cm) extra on top when working with the side of the box. Remove the colored protective foil and attach an appropriately sized piece of wrapping paper to the back of the self-adhesive tape. Cut along the lines, making sure to leave the aforementioned extra room where necessary. Remove the proof-paper on the other side of the self-adhesive tape and stick the laminated wrapping paper to the bottom and outer edge of the box, one after another, making sure there are as few wrinkles as possible. Cut the extra paper at the upper edge of the box so that it sticks up only ¹/₅ in. (5 mm) and then fold it down over the edge of the box and press down. Do the same with the lid of the box, as well. If you wish, you can stick wrapping paper to the inside of the box using the same technique.

Colorful Cookies

Marzipan Almond Crescents

Makes 2 trays

For the dough: 7 oz (200 g) marzipan paste, ½ cup + ¹/₃ cup (100 g) powdered sugar, 1 tsp gingerbread spice, 2 tsp almond syrup, 1 egg white
For decorating: 1 egg yolk, 1 tbsp orange juice, ½ cup + 1 tbsp (60 g) sliced almonds
Additional: piping bag with round tip

Preheat the oven to 340°F (170°C), unless you have a convection oven, in which case preheat to 300°F (150°C), or a gas oven, in which case preheat to level 2–3. Line two baking sheets with parchment paper.

Grate the marzipan coarsely. In a bowl, mix the marzipan, powdered sugar, gingerbread spice, almond syrup, and egg white into a smooth mass using a hand mixer with the whisk attachment. Pour into a piping bag with a round tip and squeeze 1.5 in. (4 cm) long crescents onto the baking sheet, being sure to leave space between them.

Whisk the egg yolk and orange juice together. Thinly coat the crescents with that mixture and sprinkle with sliced almonds. Bake one tray after another in the preheated oven (second shelf from the bottom) for 15 minutes, until lightly colored. Remove and let cool. Temper the couverture (see page 10–11) or melt the glaze according to the package directions and immerse the ends of the crescents. Let the excess couverture or icing drip off and place the crescents on a cooling rack so that the chocolate can harden.

Colorful Cookies

Layered Nougat Cookies

MAKES 1 TRAY

For the dough: 1½ cup + 5 tsp (200 g) flour, ¾ cup + 2 tsp (80 g) ground hazelnuts, ¾ cup (175 g) butter, ½ cup + 2 tbsp (75 g) powdered sugar, 2 tsp (8 g) vanilla sugar, zest from 1 organic orange, 1 egg yolk

For the filling and icing: ½ cup + 1 tbsp (100 g) chopped hazelnuts, 4½ oz (125 g) nougat, $^1/_3$ cup (75 g) butter, 5¼ oz (150 g) dark couverture chocolate, 3½ oz (100 g) good-quality nut glaze

Additional: flour for the countertop, parchment paper, plastic wrap

Knead flour, ground nuts, butter that has been cut into small pieces, powdered sugar, and vanilla sugar, as well as orange zest and egg yolk, into a smooth dough. Form into a ball, wrap in plastic wrap, and let sit in the refrigerator for 2 hours.

Preheat the oven to 355°F (180°C), unless you have a convection oven, in which case preheat to 320°F (160°C), or a gas oven, in which case preheat to level 3. Line a baking sheet with parchment paper. Separate the dough into several pieces and roll it out thinly on a floured countertop. Cut out rectangles or circles with wavy edges in three different sizes, making an even number of each type. Place them on the baking sheet and bake in the preheated oven (second shelf from the bottom) for 6–8 minutes. Remove and let cool.

For the filling and glaze, toast the chopped hazelnuts in a nonstick frying pan (without fat) and let cool. Mix the nougat and butter together until creamy. Stir in half of the cooled nuts. Spread the nougat mixture—not too thinly—onto the cookies of the largest and medium sizes, stack them together along with the smallest cookies, and place onto parchment paper. Chop the couverture and/or glaze and melt them together using a double boiler. Make a piping bag out of parchment paper, fill it with the frosting, and cut a small hole into the tip of the bag. Squeeze fine lines of frosting over the cookies diagonally, sprinkle with the remaining coarsely chopped nuts, and leave out to dry.

 Let the nougat cookies sit out overnight at room temperature before placing in an airtight container to ensure that the nougat filling is completely dry.

Colorful Cookies

Mini Stollen (Fruit Cake)

MAKES 1 TRAY

For the dough: 2 cups (250 g) flour, 1 tbsp milk, $^1/_3$ cup (70 g) sugar, 1½ oz (42 g) dry yeast, 4½ oz (125 g) low-fat quark, 1 pinch salt, 1 egg, $^1/_3$ cup + 2 tbsp (100 g) butter, ½ cup (75 g) raisins, 3½ oz (100 g) candied orange peel or 1¾ oz (50 g) candied orange peel and 1¾ oz (50 g) candied lemon peel, a little bit of lemon juice

For decorating: $^1/_3$ cup + 2 tbsp (100 g) butter to brush on top of the dough, ½ cup + $^1/_3$ cup (100 g) powdered sugar to sprinkle on top

In a bowl, combine flour, milk, ½ tsp sugar, and dry yeast together to form a dough, and let rise in a warm, draft-free place until cracks appear on the surface. Now knead well, along with quark, salt, egg, the remaining sugar, butter, raisins, candied orange, and/or lemon peel, and lemon juice into a firm, smooth dough. Cover and let rise in a warm, draft-free place until the volume has doubled.

Preheat the oven to 355°F (180°C), unless you have a convection oven, in which case preheat to 320°F (160°C), or a gas oven, in which case preheat to level 3. Knead the dough again, cut it in half, and roll out until it is 1 in. (2½ cm) thick, 4 in. (10 cm) wide, elongated rectangle. With the edge of your hand, make a depression in the middle. Slap the two long sides over one another, making the shape that of an elongated Stollen cookie. Cut into 2 in. (5 cm) long pieces and place them onto a lined baking tray. Let rise for another 15 minutes. Place in a preheated oven (middle rack) and bake 15–20 minutes, until golden brown. Meanwhile, melt the butter to be brushed on the dough. Remove the mini Stollen, immediately brush with the melted butter a few times, and pour powdered sugar over them until they are thickly coated.

 You can also mix the powdered sugar with vanilla sugar and then coat the mini Stollen with that mixture instead.

Colorful Cookies

Cookie Houses

Makes 1 tray

For the dough: The ingredients are the same as those in the nougat cookies (see page 50)
For the decoration: 4 egg whites, 1 pinch salt, ½ cup + 2 tbsp (125 g) sugar, ½ cup + ⅓ cup (100 g) powdered sugar, 1 tbsp + 1⅔ tsp (15 g) starch, 10½ oz (300 g) marshmallows, 3½ oz (100 g) good-quality dark chocolate glaze
Additional: flour for the countertop, 1⅔ in. x 2⅓ in. (4 cm x 6 cm) rectangular cookie cutter with a scalloped edge, parchment paper, plastic wrap

The day before you bake these cookies, prepare the dough from the nougat terrace recipe (see page 50), wrap it in plastic wrap, and refrigerate for 2 hours. Preheat the oven to 355° F (180°C), unless you have a convection oven, in which case preheat to 320°F (160°C), or a gas oven, in which case preheat to level 3. Line a baking sheet with parchment paper. Separate the dough into multiple pieces, roll those pieces out thinly on a floured countertop, and cut out rectangles. The number of rectangles you cut should be divisible by 3. Place the rectangles on the baking sheet and bake in a preheated oven (second shelf from the bottom) for 6–8 minutes. Remove and let cool.

For decorating, beat the egg whites and salt in a bowl until frothy, using a hand mixer with a whisk attachment. Sprinkle in sugar and continue mixing until the crystals have dissolved. Mix the powdered sugar and starch, sift it into the egg white mixture, and carefully fold in. Make a piping bag out of parchment paper, fill it with the egg white mass, and cut a hole at the tip. Squeeze some of the mixture onto the center of a cookie and stick a marshmallow to it. Cover the top of the marshmallows with the egg white mixture. Then use the egg white mixture to glue two cookies together on the long sides to form a roof and stick it to the marshmallow. Hold the pieces in place until the roof stays together on its own. With the rest of the ingredients, repeat the same procedure until there are no cookies left. Place the cookie houses on a lined baking sheet and let dry at room temperature overnight. Cover the remaining egg white mixture and place it in the refrigerator.

The next day, melt the chocolate glaze according to the package directions. Make two icing bags out of parchment paper, filling one with glaze and the other with the remaining egg white mixture. Cut a hole at the tip of each one. Cover the roofs of the cookie houses with zigzag lines of glaze and create decorative snow and icicles from the egg white mixture (see photo). Finally, cut the marshmallows into quarters and stick them onto the houses as chimneys, using the egg white mixture as glue.

Colorful Cookies

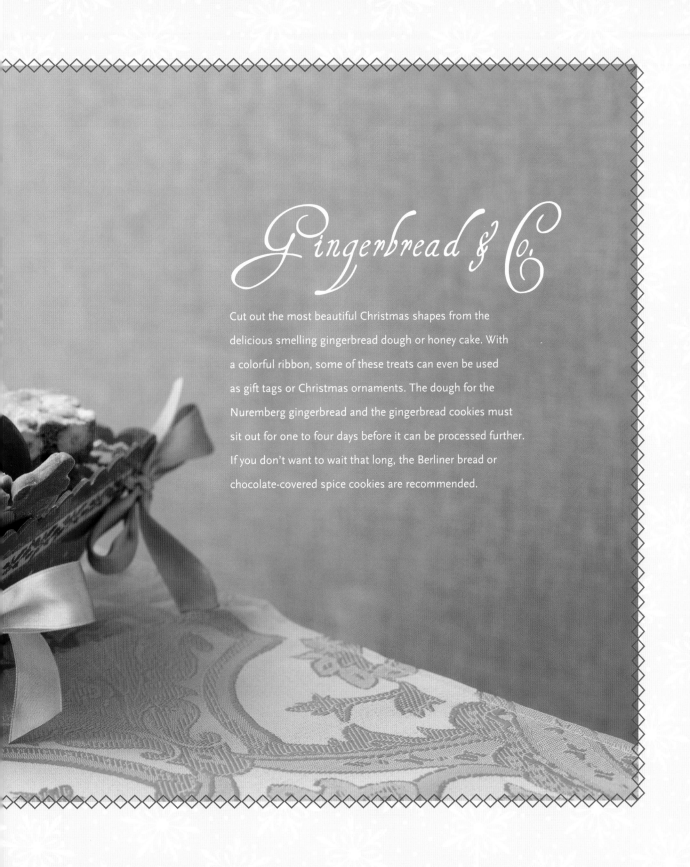

Gingerbread & Co.

Cut out the most beautiful Christmas shapes from the delicious smelling gingerbread dough or honey cake. With a colorful ribbon, some of these treats can even be used as gift tags or Christmas ornaments. The dough for the Nuremberg gingerbread and the gingerbread cookies must sit out for one to four days before it can be processed further. If you don't want to wait that long, the Berliner bread or chocolate-covered spice cookies are recommended.

Berliner Bread

MAKES 1 TRAY

For the dough: 2²/₃ oz (75 g) milk chocolate, 2 eggs, 1 cup (250 g) raw cane sugar, 2 cups (250 g) flour, 1 tsp baking powder, 2½ oz (70 g) sugar beet syrup (alternatively apple butter), 2 tbsp rum, 1 pinch allspice, 1–2 tbsp cocoa powder, 1 tbsp ground cinnamon, 1¹/₃ cup (200 g) whole hazelnuts
For the icing: ¹/₃ cup + 4 tsp (50 g) powdered sugar, 1 tbsp lemon juice
Additional: butter for the baking sheet

Grate the chocolate. Beat eggs and 2 tbsp lukewarm water in a bowl until thick and creamy while gradually sprinkling in the sugar. Mix the flour and baking powder together. Fold the sugar beet syrup, rum, allspice, cocoa powder, and cinnamon into the egg mixture. Stir in the flour mixture as well. Finally, incorporate the grated chocolate and hazelnuts with a wooden spoon.

Preheat the oven to 355°F (180°C), unless you have a convection oven, in which case preheat to 320°F (160°C), or a gas oven, in which case preheat to level 3. Butter the baking sheet. Spread out the dough so it is about ²/₅ in. (1 cm) thick and covering about two-thirds of the baking sheet. Place into the preheated oven and bake 15–20 minutes, until light brown.

Remove and immediately cut into rectangles with edges that are 2 in. x 1½ in. (5 cm x 4 cm). Mix the powdered sugar with the lemon juice until smooth and spread the rectangles with the glaze.

Gingerbread & Co.

Honey Cake

MAKES 1 TRAY

For the dough: 1½ cups (500 g) honey, ²/₃ cup (a little bit more than ¹/₈ l) vegetable oil, 1¼ cup (250 g) sugar, 5²/₃ cups (700 g) flour, 1 tbsp (10 g) baking powder, 2²/₃ (250 g) ground almonds (blanched), ½ oz (15 g) gingerbread spice, 1 pinch salt, 3 eggs, 3½ oz (100 g) finely chopped candied lemon peel, 3½ oz (100 g) finely chopped candied orange peel

For decorating: 3 tbsp condensed milk, 3½ oz (100 g) peeled maraschino cherries, ¾ cup (100 g) almonds

Additional: butter for the baking sheet, flour to knead in

In a pot over medium heat, bring the honey to a boil with the oil and sugar and let cool again. Sift the flour and the baking powder into a bowl and mix with almonds, gingerbread spice, salt, eggs, candied lemon peel, and candied orange peel. Add in the cooled honey mixture and knead everything together well. If necessary, knead in a little more flour. Leave the dough covered in the refrigerator for 1 hour.

Preheat the oven to 390°F (200°C), unless you have a convection oven, in which case preheat to 355°F (180°C), or a gas oven, in which case preheat to level 4. Grease a baking sheet. Place the dough onto the baking sheet, press down on it evenly using floured hands, and then brush with the condensed milk. Using a sharp knife and a ruler, mark 2¹/₃ in. x 2¹/₃ in. (6 cm x 6 cm) squares on the cake. Garnish each piece with a symmetrical pattern of halved maraschino cherries and peeled almonds (see photo). Place into a preheated oven (middle rack) and bake 35–45 minutes, until light brown.

Remove from the oven, let cool slightly, divide the dough into the marked squares, and let cool on a wire rack.

Gingerbread & Co.

Chocolate-Covered Spice Cookies

MAKES 2 TRAYS

For the dough: 4 eggs, 1 tsp lemon juice, 1¼ cups (150 g) powdered sugar, 1 pinch salt, zest from 1 organic lemon, 1–2 tsp gingerbread spice, 2 cups + 5 tsp (200 g) ground almonds, 2 cups (200 g) ground hazelnuts

For the base layer: 28 baking wafers (3 in. diameter [7 or 8 cm])

For the icing: 7 oz (200 g) dark couverture chocolate, 3½ oz (100 g) good-quality dark chocolate glaze

Preheat the oven to 320°F (160°C), unless you have a convection oven, in which case preheat to 285°F (140°C), or a gas oven, in which case preheat to level 2. Beat eggs, lemon juice, and powdered sugar into a thick cream using a hand mixer with a whisk attachment. Mix in the remaining dough ingredients with a wooden spoon. Place the dough onto the wafers in little dome shapes, approximately ²/₅ in. (1 cm) thick.

Put the gingerbread onto two baking sheets, place them into the preheated oven (middle rack), and bake for about 15 minutes. Remove from the oven and let cool.

Meanwhile, melt the couverture and the glaze together over a double boiler, mix well, and spread on top of the gingerbread.

Gingerbread & Co.

Nuremberg Gingerbread

Makes 1 tray

For the crust: 5 eggs, 1¾ cups (350 g) sugar, (125 g) ground almonds (blanched), ¾ cup + 1 tbsp (100 g) flour, 1¾ oz (50 g) very finely diced candied lemon peel, 1¾ oz (50 g) very finely diced candied orange peel, 2 tsp ground cinnamon, ¼ tsp ground cardamom, 1 pinch allspice, 1 pinch ground ginger

For the base layer: 28 baking wafers

For the icing: ½ cup (100 g) sugar, 1 tbsp lemon juice, 2 tbsp hot water, 2²/₃ oz (75 g) couverture dark chocolate or good-quality dark chocolate glaze, ¹/₃ cup (50 g) blanched almonds

The day before baking, use a hand mixer with a whisk attachment to beat the eggs and sugar. Do this over a hot water bath until the mixture reaches a temperature of 104°F (40°C). Remove the bowl from the hot water bath and beat until cold again. In a second bowl, mix almonds, flour, candied lemon peel, candied orange peel, cinnamon, cardamom, allspice, and ginger and carefully fold into the egg-sugar mixture. Coat the wafers with a ¾ in. (2 cm) thick layer of dough, which can be evened out using a kitchen knife that has been dipped in water. Place on a plate and allow to dry overnight at room temperature so the gingerbread cookies retain their shape when baked.

The next day, preheat the oven to 355°F (180°C), unless you have a convection oven, in which case preheat to 320°F (160°C), or a gas oven, in which case preheat to level 3. Place the baking sheet with the gingerbread cookies in the oven (middle rack) and bake for 15–20 minutes so the gingerbread is brown but still soft on the inside.

Meanwhile, for the glaze, mix sugar with lemon juice and hot water in a pot and briefly bring to a boil. Take the gingerbread cookies out of the oven and, while they are still hot, cover half of them with the glaze and place them on a wire rack to dry. Temper the couverture (see pages 10–11) or melt the chocolate glaze according to package directions. Then, after the remaining cookies have cooled, coat them with either the couverture or the chocolate glaze and decorate each with 3 peeled almond halves.

 Cover a round box with the wrapping paper of your choice (see instructions, page 46) and, as a final touch, add a pretty bow.

Gingerbread Cookies

MAKES 2 TRAYS

For the dough: 14 oz (400 g) sugar beet syrup, ¹/₃ cup + 2 tbsp (100 g) butter, ½ tbsp (10 g) potash, 4 tbsp orange juice, 4 cups (500 g) flour, ½ oz (15 g) gingerbread spice, zest from ½ of an organic lemon, 1¾ oz (50 g) diced candied lemon peel, 1¾ oz (50 g) diced candied orange peel, ½ cup (50 g) finely diced walnuts

For the icing: 2 egg whites, 3 cups + 2 tbsp (375 g) powdered sugar

Additional: flour for the countertop, assorted cookie cutters (i.e. angel, Santa's boot, rocking horse), parchment paper

Four days before baking, warm the sugar beet syrup in a pot with butter on low heat until the butter melts. Pour into a mixing bowl. Stir the potash and the orange juice until the potash dissolves and then add that into the bowl, as well. Next, add in flour, gingerbread spice, lemon zest, candied lemon peel, candied orange peel, and nuts, and knead everything into a smooth dough. Leave out, covered, for four days at room temperature. In that time, repeatedly knead the dough thoroughly.

On the day you bake the gingerbread, preheat the oven to 390°F (200°C), unless you have a convection oven, in which case preheat to 355°F (180°C), or a gas oven, in which case preheat to level 4. Separate the dough into pieces and roll them out until they are approximately ¹/₅ in. (4 mm) thick on the floured countertop. Cut out assorted shapes using cookie cutters and place onto baking sheets lined with parchment paper. Place the baking sheets in the preheated oven (middle rack) and bake the gingerbread cookies for 10–15 minutes. Remove the cookies from the parchment paper while they are still hot and let cool on a wire rack.

Afterward, beat the egg whites to stiff peaks. Add powdered sugar while you beat—use an amount that will ensure the mixture is thick enough to be squeezed from a tube. Make a piping bag out of parchment paper, fill it with the icing, and cut a small hole in the tip of the bag. Then decorate the gingerbread cookies by squeezing the icing onto them in fine lines (see photo) and let dry.

You can also make holes in the gingerbread cookies, put ribbons through them, and use them as edible decorations on gifts or as Christmas ornaments.

Gingerbread & Co.

Gingerbread Christmas Ornaments

MAKES 2 TRAYS

For the dough: ¹/₃ cup + 2 tbsp (100 g) butter, ¾ cup (250 g) honey, ½ cup + 2 tbsp (125 g) sugar, ¼ oz (7½ g) gingerbread spice, 1½ tbsp (8 g) cocoa powder, 4¾ cups + 2 tsp (600 g) flour, 2 tsp (7½ g) baking powder, 1 pinch salt, 1 egg
For the icing: 2 egg whites, 3 cups + 2 tbsp (375 g) powdered sugar
Additional: flour for the countertop, assorted cookie cutters (heart, star, etc.), parchment paper, ribbon, aluminum foil

On the day before baking, heat the butter with honey, sugar, gingerbread spice, and cocoa in a saucepan over low heat. Stir constantly until the sugar has completely dissolved. Remove from heat and let cool.

Sift the flour and baking powder into a bowl with the honey mixture, salt, and egg and knead into a smooth dough. Form the dough into a ball, wrap in aluminum foil, cover with a bowl, and leave out at room temperature overnight.

The next day, preheat the oven to 390°F (200°C), unless you have a convection oven, in which case preheat to 355°F (180°C), or a gas oven, in which case preheat to level 4. Roll out the dough a piece at a time on a floured work surface until it is uniformly ¹/₅ in. (4 mm) thick. Use cookie cutters to cut out pieces of gingerbread and place them on baking sheets lined with parchment paper. With a needle, make a hole at the top of each cut-out piece of gingerbread so that ribbon can be pulled through it later. Place the baking sheets in the preheated oven (middle rack) and bake the gingerbread for 12–15 minutes. Remove from the parchment paper while still hot and let cool on a wire rack.

Afterward, beat the egg whites to stiff peaks. Add powdered sugar while you beat—use an amount that will ensure the mixture is thick enough to be squeezed from a tube. Make a piping bag out of parchment paper, fill it with the icing, and cut a small hole in the tip of the bag. Decorate the gingerbread with symmetrical patterns (see photo) and let dry. Pull a piece of ribbon through each hole and use the pieces of gingerbread as Christmas ornaments.

Gingerbread & Co.

Gingerbread Puzzle

MAKES 2 TRAYS

For the dough: ingredients are the same as those in the gingerbread Christmas tree recipe (see page 68)

For decorating: 1²/₃ cup (200 g) powdered sugar, 2–3 tbsp lemon juice, green food coloring, bright sugar pearls

Additional: butter for the baking pan, large Christmas tree cookie cutter (at least 4 in. [10 cm] lengthwise), flour for the countertop, parchment paper

The day before baking, prepare the gingerbread dough according to the recipe (see page 68) and let it rest overnight at room temperature.

The next day, preheat the oven to 355°F (180°C), unless you have a convection oven, in which case preheat to 320°F (160°C), or a gas oven, in which case preheat to level 3. Grease both baking sheets. If you do not have a Christmas tree cookie cutter on hand, you can instead make a Christmas tree template. Roll out the dough ¹/₅ in. (½ cm) thick on a floured surface, use the cookie cutter to cut out the Christmas trees or lay down the template and cut out the Christmas trees using a knife. Then cut the Christmas trees into five puzzle pieces. Put the puzzle pieces on the baking sheets and bake one after another in the preheated oven (middle rack) for 12–15 minutes. Remove from the oven and let cool on a wire rack.

In a bowl, mix the powdered sugar with the lemon juice to form a mixture thick enough to be squeezed from a tube. Leave one-third of the mixture white, but dye the rest of the mixture green using food coloring. Spread the puzzle pieces with green icing and let dry. Make a piping bag out of parchment paper, fill it with the white icing, and cut a small hole in the tip of the bag. Put the puzzle pieces together so that they once again form trees and decorate with fine lines of white icing and sugar pearls.

Gingerbread & Co.

Springerle Cookies

MAKES 1 TRAY

For the dough: 2 eggs, 2 cups + 4 tsp (250 g) powdered sugar, ½ tsp vanilla sugar, 1 pinch salt, zest from ½ organic lemon, 2 cups (250 g) flour
Additional: 1 tsp anise powder, springerle mold, flour to knead in, aluminum foil, brush

The day before baking, stir eggs and powdered sugar together in a bowl using a hand mixer with the whisk attachment until foamy. Gradually mix in vanilla sugar, salt, lemon zest, and sifted flour and then stir using the dough hook.

Line a baking sheet with parchment paper and sprinkle with anise powder. Knead half the dough thoroughly on a floured countertop and roll it out so that it is $^2/_5$ in. (1 cm) thick. Cover the bowl filled with excess dough so that it does not dry out. Sprinkle the wooden mold with flour and then sprinkle the dough with a little flour, as well. Press a small piece of dough into the mold and take it out again. Cut along the edges of the image using a knife or a pastry wheel, remove the excess dough, and place the cookie on the baking sheet. Repeat this process with the remaining dough. Cover the baking sheet with a kitchen towel and let the Springerle cookies sit at room temperature for 24 hours.

On the day you will bake the cookies, preheat the oven to 320°F (160°C), unless you have a convection oven, in which case preheat to 285°F (140°C), or a gas oven, in which case preheat to level 2. Place the baking sheets in the preheated oven (middle rack) and bake the Springerle cookies for about 20 minutes, until they are very lightly colored. If needed, cover with aluminum foil after 15 minutes. Remove from the baking sheet, remove the flour residue with a brush, and allow the Springerle cookies to cool on a wire rack.

 You should bake the Springerle cookies about three weeks before they are to be consumed so that they can develop their full flavor. Up until they are eaten, it is best to store them in an airtight container.

Lebkuchen & Co.

Three Types of Aachener Printen

FOR 2 TRAYS

For the dough: (250 g) sugar beet syrup, 1 level tsp potash, ¼ cup (50 g) granulated brown sugar, 2²/₃ oz (75 g) coarse white rock sugar, 2¹/₃ cups + 1 tbsp (300 g) flour, 1 tsp ground cinnamon, 1 tsp ground anise, ½ tsp ground ginger, ¼ tsp ground cloves, ¼ tsp ground coriander, ¼ tsp ground allspice

For decorating: ½ cup milk, ½ cup + 2 tsp (50 g) slivered almonds, 7 oz (200 g) dark couverture chocolate

Additional: flour for the countertop

Two to three days before baking, boil the sugar beet syrup in a pot with 2 tbsp water. Mix the potash with 1 tbsp water and add it in. Stir in the granulated brown sugar and the rock sugar. Allow to cool, stirring occasionally. Mix in the flour and the spices. Let the dough sit out at room temperature, covered, for two to three days.

On the day you will bake the Aachener Printen, preheat the oven to 355°F (180°C), unless you have a convection oven, in which case preheat to 320°F (160°C), or a gas oven, in which case preheat to level 3. Knead the dough thoroughly, and roll out on a floured work surface about ¹/₅ in. (5 mm) thick. Cut out rectangles of approximately 3 in. x 1 in. (8 cm x 3 cm). Brush with milk. Place slivered almonds onto one-third of gingerbread. Then put all of the gingerbread on lined baking sheets, and bake in the preheated oven for about 15 minutes. Remove from the baking sheets and let cool. Spread the tempered couverture (see pages 10–11) onto the Aachener Printen with almonds, as well as half of the remaining gingerbread, and let cool.

 For the decorative Christmas box, you need a white box, double-sided tape, and wrapping paper of your choice. Trace the bottom of the box, as well as the four sides, onto some proof-paper. Leave ²/₅ in. (1 cm) extra on the upper edges when working with the sides of the box so you are able to turn the edges of the paper down. In addition, add another centimeter in length to two sides of the box. Attach an appropriately sized piece of wrapping paper to a piece of tape. Cut along the marked lines, making sure to include the additions, cutting from the top of them, all the way to the bottom of the box. First cover the bottom of the box by removing the proof-paper and attaching the wrapping paper carefully and exactly. Stick the pages that have the ⁴/₅ in. (2 cm) additions on them on the box, fold down each of these, and press down on them. Then attach the pages with the smaller additions, turn down the extra on top, and press down. Proceed in the same way with the lid.

Lebkuchen & Co.

Almond Speculoos Cookies

MAKES 2 TRAYS

For the dough: 1 cup + 1½ tbsp (250 g) butter, 1½ cup (300 g) sugar, 3½ oz (100 g) marzipan paste, 1 egg, 4 cups (500 g) flour, 1 pinch salt, ½ oz (15 g) gingerbread spice
Additional: flour for the mold and baking sheets, ¾ cup + 3 tbsp (100 g) flaked almonds, spatula, aluminum foil

Knead the butter with sugar and marzipan. Then knead in the egg, sifted flour, salt, and gingerbread spice. Form the dough into a ball, wrap in aluminum foil, and let stand in the refrigerator for 2 hours.

Preheat the oven to 390°F (200°C), unless you have a convection oven, in which case preheat to 355°F (180°C), or a gas oven, in which case preheat to level 4. Dust the mold and the baking sheets with flour, and sprinkle the baking sheets with flaked almonds. Roll out the dough on a floured countertop until it is just under ¹/₅ in. (½ cm) thick.

Cut off small pieces of the dough and press them into the mold. Cut off the extra dough from around the edges. Hit the backside of the mold hard to release the dough and let it fall onto the baking sheets.

Place the baking sheets in the preheated oven (middle rack) one after another and bake for about 10 minutes. Afterward, the almonds should be golden. Immediately remove the cookies from the baking sheet with a spatula and place them onto a wire rack to cool.

Lebkuchen & Co.

International Specialties

Looking out over the edge of the German cookie plate and peering into those of other countries is definitely worth your while: The Swiss love their Basler Brunsli (chocolate almond spice cookies) and fine creations like the Zurich Tirggel (honey cookies). The Austrians have created delicious Christmas specialties such as filled Linzer cookies and poppyseed plum pockets. More typical Christmas pastry products come out of Italian bakeries, such as Panforte (fruitcake) or Zaleti (cornmeal cookies). A wide variety of inspirations for Advent baking can also be found in the Anglo-Saxon world in desserts such as Christmas cookies, brownie Christmas trees, and shortbread hearts.

Zurich Tirggel (Honey Cookies)

MAKES 1 TRAY

For the dough: 2^1/$_3$ cups (800 g) honey, 5¾ tbsp (30 g) ground ginger, 4 tbsp (30 g) ground cinnamon, ¾ tbsp (5 g) ground cloves, ¾ tbsp (5 g) freshly grated nutmeg, 1 pinch allspice, 2 tbsp rosewater, 6^1/$_3$ cups (a little less than 800 g) flour

Additional: flour for the countertop, wooden mold, oil and flour for the mold, spatula

Mix honey with ginger, cinnamon, cloves, nutmeg, allspice and rosewater in a double boiler. Slowly add in flour until the dough detaches from the edge of the bowl.

Preheat the oven to 535°F (280°C), unless you have a convection oven, in which case preheat to the maximum temperature, or a gas oven, in which case preheat to level 10. Lightly grease and flour the baking sheet. Roll out the dough onto a floured countertop until it is about ^{1}/$_{10}$ in. (2 mm) thick. Grease the small wooden mold with oil, sprinkle some flour on it, and press the dough into it. Carefully remove the dough from the mold and place it on the baking sheet.

Place the baking sheet in the oven (top rack) and bake the Tirggel until they take on a delicate light brown color. Remove them from the baking sheet with a spatula and place them on a wire rack to cool.

Basel Biscuits (Hard Spice Bars)

MAKES 1 TRAY

For the dough: $^2/_3$ cup (100 g) blanched almonds, $^2/_3$ cup (100 g) shelled hazelnuts, 1 cup (100 g) shelled walnuts, 4½ oz (125 g) candied orange peel, 4½ oz (125 g) candied lemon peel, 1 cup (350 g) honey, 1¼ cup (250 g) sugar, 4 cups (500 g) flour, 4 tbsp (30 g) ground cinnamon, zest from 1 organic lemon, 2 pinches ground cloves, 1 pinch freshly ground nutmeg, 2 tsp potash, 2 tsp hartshorn salt, 1 tbsp + 1 tsp (2 cl) arrack, 1 tbsp + 1 tsp (2 cl) cherry brandy
For the icing: ½ cup (100 g) sugar
Additional: butter for the baking sheet, flour for the countertop

Finely chop almonds, hazelnuts, walnuts, candied orange peel, and candied lemon peel, and place into a bowl. In a pot, bring honey and sugar to a boil while stirring. Sift the flour into the chopped ingredients and mix in with the hot honey mixture and spices, along with potash and hartshorn salt. Mix in the arrack and cherry brandy. Form the dough into a ball, cover with a bowl, and let stand at room temperature for 3–4 hours.

Then preheat the oven to 390°F (200°C), unless you have a convection oven, in which case preheat to 355°F (180°C), or a gas oven, in which case preheat to level 4. Grease the baking sheet. Roll out the dough to the size of the baking sheet, with a thickness of about $^2/_5$ in. (1 cm), on a floured countertop. Then place the dough onto the baking sheet. Put the baking sheet into the preheated oven (middle rack), and bake for 15–20 minutes.

Meanwhile, for the icing, boil the sugar with a little bit of water in a pot and set aside. Take the baking sheet out of the oven, spread the Basel biscuits with icing immediately, and cut into 2 in x 1¼ in. (5 cm x 3 cm) rectangles.

Basler Brunsli (Chocolate Almond Spice Cookies)

Makes 1 tray

For the dough: (200 g) dark chocolate, 2 egg whites, 5¼ cups (500 g) ground almonds, 2 cups (400 g) sugar, 2 tbsp unsweetened cocoa powder, ½ tsp ground cinnamon, 1 pinch freshly ground mace, 3 tbsp cherry brandy

Additional: coarse sugar for the countertop, butter for the baking sheet, assorted cookie cutters (i.e. star, heart, clover)

Grate the chocolate very finely using a grater. Beat the egg whites to stiff peaks using a hand mixer with the whisk attachment. In a bowl, mix the chocolate with the almonds, sugar, cocoa powder, cinnamon, mace, and cherry brandy, and knead thoroughly. Carefully fold in the beaten egg white.

Sprinkle the countertop with coarse sugar and roll out the dough on top of it until it is $^2/_5$ in. (1 cm) thick. Cut out cookies with the assorted cookie cutters and place them onto a well greased baking sheet, leaving at least the width of a finger between each cookie. Let harden for at least 2 hours at room temperature.

Next, preheat the oven to 355°F (180°C), unless you have a convection oven, in which case preheat to 320°F (160°C), or a gas oven, in which case preheat to level 3. Place the Brunsli in the oven and bake for approximately 5 minutes. After this amount of time, they should have a bit more of a crust, but should not have changed color at all. Take the cookies out of the oven and, after letting them sit out for 2–3 minutes, remove them from the baking sheet carefully and set on a wire rack to cool. When they are fully cooled, store them in airtight containers.

Chocolate Cassis Pockets

Makes 1 tray

For the dough: 1 cup + 3 tbsp (150 g) flour, 1 pinch baking powder, 2 tbsp + 2$^1/_3$ tsp (15 g) cocoa powder, $^1/_3$ cup + 2 tsp (75 g) sugar, 1 pinch salt, 1 egg, $^1/_3$ cup + 2 tbsp (100 g) soft butter

For the cassis filling: 10$^2/_3$ oz (300 g) black currant jam, ½ tsp locust bean gum (plant-based binding agent, found in health-food stores)

For the icing: 1¾ oz (50 g) white couverture chocolate or good-quality white chocolate glaze

Additional: flour to knead in, plastic wrap

Sift flour, baking powder, and cocoa powder into a bowl. Rapidly incorporate the sugar, salt, egg, and butter using the dough hook of the hand mixer. As soon as those ingredients are mixed in, immediately start kneading the mixture into a smooth dough using your hands on a lightly floured countertop. Once the dough is smooth, form it into a ball, wrap it in plastic wrap, and let it rest for 3 hours in the refrigerator.

Meanwhile, for the filling, sift the jam into a bowl and bind with the locust bean gum.

Preheat the oven to 355°F (180°C), unless you have a convection oven, in which case pre-heat to 320°F (160°C), or a gas oven, in which case preheat to level 3. Line a baking sheet with parchment paper. Roll out the dough on a floured surface until it is $^1/_{10}$ in. (3 mm) thick. Then cut out right triangles with legs 2 in. (5 cm) long using a pastry wheel and a straight edge. Place ½ tsp cassis filling in the middle of half of the triangles and then place the leftover, plain triangles on top. Press the edges together using the back of a knife, and then put the chocolate cassis pockets onto the baking sheet. Place the baking sheet in a preheated oven (middle rack) and bake for 13–15 minutes. Take out of the oven, remove the pockets along with the parchment paper from the baking sheets and let cool.

Temper the couverture (see pages 10–11) or melt the chocolate glaze according to the package directions. Dip one corner of each pocket into the chocolate that you chose. Let dry on a wire rack.

International Specialties

Filled Linzer Cookies

MAKES 1 TRAY

For the dough: 1 cup (220 g) soft butter, ²/₃ cup (80 g) powdered sugar, 1 tbsp vanilla sugar, 1 pinch salt, a little bit of organic lemon zest, 1 egg, 1 egg yolk, 1 cup + 3 tbsp (150 g) flour, 1¼ cups (150 g) coarse-grained flour (alternatively instant flour)
For the filling: approx. 3½ oz (100 g) strawberry jam
For the icing: 7 oz (200 g) dark couverture chocolate or good-quality dark chocolate glaze
Additional: parchment paper, piping bag with tip number 6 (round)

In a bowl, beat butter, powdered sugar, vanilla sugar, salt, and lemon zest until fluffy. In a smaller bowl, beat the egg and egg yolk together, and then stir that into the butter-sugar mixture. Mix the two types of flour together and fold into the main mixture.

Preheat the oven to 390°F (200°C), unless you have a convection oven, in which case pre-heat to 355°F (180°C), or a gas oven, in which case preheat to level 4. Line a baking sheet with parchment paper. Fill a piping bag with dough and squeeze little mounds onto the parchment paper, making sure to leave sufficient room between them. Place in the preheated oven (middle rack) and bake for 10 minutes, until very lightly colored.

Remove the cookies from the oven and let cool. Turn over half of the Linzers, brush them with jam, and place the leftover cookies on top.

Temper the couverture (see pages 10–11) or melt the chocolate glaze according to the package directions. Dunk about one-third of each Linzer into the type of chocolate that you chose, put them on a wire rack, and let dry.

International Specialties

Poppyseed Plum Cake

MAKES 1 TRAY

For the dough: 6 eggs, 2 egg whites, ¾ cup + 2½ tbsp (180 g) sugar, 2¾ oz (80 g) freshly ground poppy seeds, zest from 1 organic lemon, 1 pinch salt, (30 g) ground almonds, ¾ cup (90 g) flour
For the filling: 7 oz (200 g) plum jam, rum as desired
For decorating: 1 organic lemon, ¼ cup (50 g) sugar, ½ cup + ⅓ cup (100 g) powdered sugar
Additional: parchment paper, sugar for sprinkling on top

Preheat the oven to 355°F (180°C), unless you have a convection oven, in which case preheat to 320°F (160°C), or a gas oven, in which case preheat to level 3. Separate 4 eggs. In a bowl, beat 2 eggs, 4 egg yolks, and ½ cup + 1 tbsp (110 g) of sugar until creamy. Mix in poppy seeds, lemon zest, salt, almonds, and flour. Beat the remaining 6 egg whites with the rest of the sugar until stiff peaks form, and then fold in gently. Line a baking sheet with parchment paper and spread the dough out so it covers approximately two-thirds of the tray. Place into a preheated oven (middle rack), and bake the dough for about 15–20 minutes, until it is light brown. Take out of the oven, sprinkle sugar on a kitchen towel, throw the kitchen towel over the dough, and let cool completely.

For the filling, bring the plum jam to a boil in a pot and stir in rum to taste. Cut the cake down the middle horizontally using a sharp knife. Coat one half of the sheet of dough with the plum jam and place the other half of the dough on top. With a sharp knife, cut into ¾ in. x 1 in. (2 cm x 2 ½ cm) pieces.

For the decoration, rinse the lemon in hot water and cut very fine pieces of zest from it. Squeeze out the juice from one half of the fruit and set aside. In a pot, bring the sugar to a boil with 50 ml of water, add in the zest, and let cook for 12–15 minutes, until tender. Remove from the pot and drain using a sieve. In a small bowl, mix the sifted powdered sugar with a little lemon juice to form a spreadable glaze. Spread the pieces of cake with the glaze and garnish with lemon zest.

♥ Those who would prefer something not quite as sweet can leave out the frosting and lemon zest and instead lightly sprinkle the cake slices with fine sugar.

International Specialties

Shortbread Hearts with Cranberries

MAKES 1 TRAY

For the dough: 1^1/$_3$ cup (300 g) salted butter, 1 cup (200 g) sugar, 4 cups (500 g) spelt flour or wheat flour, 5 oz (140 g) dried cranberries (not too finely chopped)

Additional: flour for the countertop, heart-shaped cookie cutter, parchment paper

Preheat the oven to 355°F (180°C), unless you have a convection oven, in which case preheat to 320°F (160°C), or a gas oven, in which case preheat to level 3. In a mixing bowl, beat the butter using a hand mixer with a whisk attachment for about 10 minutes. Afterward, the mixture should be creamy white and should have visibly increased in volume. Sprinkle the sugar in and continue stirring until the crystals have dissolved. Add in the flour and the cranberries and knead into a smooth dough.

Roll dough out onto a floured countertop to form a sheet approximately ^{2}/$_5$ in. (1 cm) thick. Using cookie cutters, cut out small hearts, and place onto a baking sheet lined with parchment paper.

Place the baking sheet in a preheated oven (middle rack) and bake the shortbread hearts for about 10 minutes, until they are very lightly colored. Remove the cookies from the oven, take them off the baking sheet along with the parchment paper, and allow to cool.

International Specialties

Angel Messages

MAKES 1 TRAY

For the dough: ²/₃ cup (150 g) butter, ¹/₃ cup + 4 tsp (50 g) powdered sugar, 1 tsp vanilla sugar, 1 pinch salt, ¼ cup (50 g) sour cream, 2 cups + 3 tbsp (275 g) flour
Additional: 1 alphabet embossing set (specialty store or Internet), flour to knead in, cookie cutters (i.e. wings, rectangles with wavy edges), plastic wrap

In a bowl, mix butter, powdered sugar, vanilla sugar, and salt. Slowly incorporate the sour cream and flour, and knead everything into a smooth dough. Form the dough into a ball, wrap it in plastic wrap, and let it sit in the refrigerator for 1 hour.

Preheat the oven to 375°F (190°C), unless you have a convection oven, in which case preheat to 340°F (170°C), or a gas oven, in which case preheat to level 3–4. Line a baking sheet with parchment paper. Prepare the alphabet embossing set to stamp a message of your choice. Roll out the dough on a floured countertop until it is ¹/₁₀ in. (3 mm) thick. Use cookie cutters to cut shapes out of the dough and stamp the prepared messages into the cookies.

Lay the cookies on a baking sheet, place into the preheated oven (middle rack), and bake for 7–10 minutes, until very lightly colored. Remove from the oven, pull off the baking sheet along with the parchment paper, and allow to cool.

International Specialties

Christmas Cookies

MAKES 1 TRAY

For the dough: 3½ oz (100 g) mixed nuts if desired, 5¼ oz (150 g) assorted dried fruits if desired, 1¾ cups (225 g) flour, 2 tsp baking powder, 1 pinch freshly ground nutmeg, ½ tsp gingerbread spice, $^1/_3$ cup + 1¾ tbsp (110 g) dark raw cane sugar, ½ cup (110 g) ice cold butter in cubes, 2 large eggs, 2 tbsp cream sherry or brandy (or alternatively, milk)
To sprinkle on top: dark raw cane sugar
Additional: butter for the baking sheet

Finely chop the nuts and dried fruit, separately, and set aside. Sift flour and baking powder into a large mixing bowl. Mix the spices and the sugar together. Integrate the cubes of butter into the flour using your fingertips so that a crumbly mixture forms. Beat the eggs in a bowl and add in the sherry (or brandy, or milk respectively), chopped nuts, and dried fruit. Combine all ingredients together with a wooden spoon to form a homogeneous dough.

Preheat the oven to 355°F (180°C), unless you have a convection oven, in which case preheat to 320°F (160°C), or a gas oven, in which case preheat to level 3. Place the dough on the greased baking sheet a tablespoon at a time, being sure to leave plenty of space between the cookies. With the back of a fork, press down lightly on the mounds of dough to make them slightly flat. Sprinkle each of them with cane sugar.

Place the baking sheet in the preheated oven and bake 12–15 minutes, until the cookies are golden brown. Remove from the oven and let cool on the baking sheet for 2 minutes. Then place the cookies on a wire rack and let cool completely.

Snowcaps

MAKES 1 TRAY

For the dough: 3½ oz (100 g) dark couverture chocolate, ¼ cup (50 g) butter, ¹/₃ cup (60 g) fine sugar, 1 egg, 1 egg yolk, ¾ cup + 1 tbsp (100 g) flour, 1 tbsp cocoa powder, ¼ tsp baking powder, salt, 1 tsp ground cinnamon
To roll the cookies in: ½ cup (60 g) powdered sugar

Finely chop the chocolate. Place it in a small bowl with the butter, and let melt over a hot water bath. Pour into a mixing bowl and let cool. Mix in the sugar, egg, and egg yolk. Then fold in the flour, cocoa powder, baking powder, 1 pinch of salt, and cinnamon. Let the dough rest, covered, for 2 hours in the refrigerator.

Preheat the oven to 355°F (180°C), unless you have a convection oven, in which case preheat to 320°F (160°C), or a gas oven, in which case preheat to level 3. Line a baking sheet with parchment paper. Pour some powdered sugar onto a flat plate. Shape the dough into walnut-sized balls and roll each one in the powdered sugar. Place the balls on the baking sheet, making sure to leave at least 1½ in. (4 cm) between each of the cookies. Put the baking sheet into the preheated oven (second shelf from the bottom) and bake for about 14 minutes. Remove and let cool slightly. Carefully remove from the baking sheet and let cool on a wire rack.

Peanut Butter Cookies

MAKES 1 TRAY

For the dough: 1 large egg, ½ cup (115 g) soft butter, ½ cup (125 g) crunchy peanut butter, ½ cup + 1 tbsp (140 g) raw cane sugar, ½ tsp vanilla extract, 2 tsp baking powder, 1¾ cup + ¾ tbsp (225 g) flour
For decorating: 1½ cups (200 g) roasted unsalted peanuts
Additional: butter for the baking sheet

Whisk the egg lightly in a bowl. Add in butter, peanut butter, sugar, vanilla extract, and flour mixed with baking powder. Mix everything together into a flat dough. Add flour and mix with a wooden spoon until smooth. Place the peanuts on a flat plate.

Preheat the oven to 355°F (180°C), unless you have a convection oven, in which case preheat to 320°F (160°C), or a gas oven, in which case preheat to level 3. Use a tablespoon to scoop up walnut-sized pieces of dough and roll them between your palms, making uniformly sized balls. Roll in the peanuts until completely covered. Place the balls on a greased baking sheet and flatten them slightly, making sure to leave room between each of them. Bake the cookies in the preheated oven for 12–15 minutes, until golden brown.

Remove from the oven and let cool on the baking sheet until they have hardened. Then let cool completely on a wire rack.

Walnut Espresso Cookies

MAKES 1 TRAY

For the dough: ¹/₃ cup + 2 tbsp (100 g) soft butter, ¹/₃ cup (70 g) fine sugar, ½ whisked egg, ¾ cup + 2 tbsp (110 g) flour, 1 tsp baking powder, 1–2 tsp instant espresso powder, ¹/₃ cup (40 g) finely chopped walnuts
As desired: additional chopped walnuts to roll the cookies in
Additional: parchment paper

Cream the butter and sugar in a mixing bowl. Stir in 1 egg followed by the flour mixed with baking powder. Fold in espresso powder and walnuts one after another.

Preheat the oven to 355°F (180°C), unless you have a convection oven, in which case pre-heat to 320°F (160°C), or a gas oven, in which case preheat to level 3. Use a tablespoon to scoop up small mounds of dough. Press them flat, roll them carefully in the chopped wal-nuts if so desired, and place them on a baking sheet lined with parchment paper, making sure to leave sufficient distance between them. Place the baking sheet into the preheated oven and bake for about 10 minutes. Afterward, the cookies should have taken on a little bit of color around the edges.

Remove them from the oven and let them harden for a few minutes on the baking sheet. Then place onto a wire rack and let cool completely.

International Specialties

Mini Christmas Cupcakes

Makes 1 mini-muffin pan (with 36 mini-muffins)

For the dough: 1¹/₃ cup (200 g) chopped sultanas, 1¹/₃ cup (200 g) chopped raisins, ¾ cup (120 g) chopped currants, 4¼ oz (120 g) chopped candied cranberries, 4¼ fluid oz (¹/₈ l) brandy or rum, ½ cup + 1 tbsp (125 g) butter, ½ cup + 2 tsp (110 g) granulated brown Mascobado sugar, 1 tbsp apricot jam, 1 tbsp honey, 1 tsp zest from an organic lemon or orange, 2 eggs, 1¹/₃ cup + 2 tbsp (180 g) flour, ½ tsp ground ginger, ½ tsp cinnamon, ½ tsp gingerbread spice

For the frosting: 1 egg white, 2 cups + 4 tsp (250 g) powdered sugar, 2–3 tsp lemon juice

Additional: butter for the pan, gold and pink sugar pearls for garnishing

The day before baking, put dried fruit in a bowl, fill up the bowl with brandy or rum, and let it sit out, covered, overnight.

The next day, preheat the oven to 300°F (150°C), unless you have a convection oven, in which case preheat to 265°F (130°C), or a gas oven, in which case preheat to level 1. Grease the 36 cups of the mini-muffin pan.

In a bowl, mix butter and sugar together with a hand mixer until creamy. Mix in the jam, honey, and lemon or orange zest. Add the eggs one after another and mix them in well. Add the dried fruit that has been soaking, the flour, and the spices into the butter mixture a little at a time, alternating between which ingredient is being added. Distribute the dough amongst the mini muffin cups. Each cup should be filled to the brim and smooth on top. Place into the preheated oven (middle rack), and bake the cupcakes for about 40 minutes (test with a toothpick!). Remove from the oven, allow to cool in the pan, flip over onto a wire rack, and turn the cupcakes over again.

For the frosting, lightly beat the egg white with a wooden spoon. Gradually add the sifted powdered sugar and mix together into a smooth paste. Slowly squeeze in lemon juice until the mixture becomes a little bit more fluid. Use a spatula to spread icing on every cupcake, letting a little bit spill over onto the sides, and then decorate with sugar pearls.

International Specialties

Christmas Tree Brownies

MAKES 1 TRAY

For the dough: 6 oz (170 g) dark couverture chocolate, 1 cup + 1½ tbsp (250 g) butter, 6 eggs, 1¼ cup (250 g) sugar, 1 tsp vanilla extract, 1 pinch salt, 1¾ cups (220 g) flour, 2 cups (200 g) ground hazelnuts

To dust on top: 3 tbsp powdered sugar

Additional: parchment paper, sugar, 3-star cookie cutters (small, medium, and large) sugar, aluminum foil

Finely chop the chocolate. Melt it together with the butter in a pot over low heat. Place eggs, sugar, vanilla extract, and salt in a mixing bowl. Using a hand mixer with a whisk attachment, mix for 8–10 minutes, until thick and creamy. Stir in the couverture mixture and then the flour and the nuts.

Preheat the oven to 355°F (180°C), unless you have a gas oven, in which case preheat to level 3. (Convection ovens are unsuitable for this recipe!) Spread the dough into a deep baking sheet, about 13 in. x 15 in. (32 cm x 39 cm) in size, that has been lined with parchment paper. If your baking sheet is larger, use multiple sheets of folded aluminum foil to limit the area to the correct size. Place in a preheated oven (second shelf from the bottom) and bake 15–18 minutes.

Remove the baking sheet from the oven. Let the sheet of dough cool down a bit on the baking sheet until it is only somewhat warm. Then flip over the sheet of brownie onto a properly sized, pre-cut piece of parchment paper. Sprinkle some sugar onto a flat plate. Using the cookie cutters, cut out stars of three different sizes from the still warm sheet of brownie. Dip the cookie cutters in the sugar just before cutting out each brownie. Stack one large star, one medium star and one small star on top of each other to make a tree (see photo). Repeat this process until all of the brownie is used up. Dust the trees with powdered sugar.

Almond Biscotti

MAKES 1 TRAY

For the dough: 4$^{1}/_{3}$ oz (125 g) almonds, ¼ tsp baking powder, 1$^{1}/_{3}$ cup + 1 tbsp (175 g) flour, ¾ cup (75 g) ground almonds, 1 cup (200 g) sugar, 1 pinch salt, 2 eggs
Additional: butter and flour for the baking sheet

Blanch the whole almonds in boiling water, drain in a colander, briefly let cool, and peel off the skin. Put the almonds in a pan without any fat, place the pan on the stove, and leave it there for a few minutes, more to dry the almonds than to roast them. Knead a firm dough out of the baking powder and flour mixed together, ground almonds, sugar, salt, and eggs. Gradually incorporate the whole almonds.

Preheat the oven to 300°F (150°C), unless you have a convection oven, in which case preheat to 265°F (130°C), or a gas oven, in which case preheat to level 1. Grease and lightly flour a baking sheet. Form the dough into cylindrical rolls with a diameter of 1¼ in. x 1½ in. (3 cm–4 cm) and place them on a baking sheet, making sure to leave enough distance between each roll. Put the baking sheet in the preheated oven and bake for 7–8 minutes.

Remove from the oven, cut the rolls diagonally with a very sharp knife into $^{2}/_{5}$ in.–$^{3}/_{5}$ in. (1 cm–1½ cm) thick slices, and place back onto the baking sheet, cut-side down. Slide back into the oven and bake 10 more minutes, until golden.

International Specialties

Amaretti Biscuits

MAKES 1 TRAY

For the dough: 8¾ oz (250 g) marzipan paste, 1 cup + 1½ tbsp (220 g) sugar, 1 pinch salt, ⅓ cup + 1½ tbsp (40 g) ground almonds (blanched), zest from ½ organic lemon, 3 egg whites
To sprinkle on top: 3 tbsp coarse sugar, 3 tbsp sugar
Additional: parchment paper, piping bag with tip number 6 (round)

Ideally, the day before baking, knead marzipan, sugar, and salt together on a countertop. Incorporate the almonds and lemon zest. Place the mass in a mixing bowl, add the egg whites one after another, and stir with a wooden spoon.

Line a baking sheet with parchment paper. Place the mixture into a piping bag and pipe small circles onto the parchment paper, making sure they are not too close together. Sprinkle with both coarse sugar and regular sugar. Let dry at room temperature for at least 4 hours, but preferably overnight.

Then preheat the oven to 300°F (150°C), unless you have a convection oven, in which case preheat to 265°F (130°C), or a gas oven, in which case preheat to level 1. Place the baking sheet in the oven and bake the cookies for 15 minutes. Remove Amaretti from the oven, place on a wire rack, and let cool.

♥ You should not spend too long kneading the marzipan, as this draws out the oil contained in the almond paste.

♥ It is recommended to bake a few sample Amaretti biscuits to test whether the dough spreads out too much during baking. If that is the case, add in more ground almonds.

Panforte Wedges

Makes 3 mini springform pans (diameter 6 in. [15 cm])

For the dough: $^2/_3$ cup (100 g) hazelnuts, ¾ cup (100 g) almonds, 5¼ oz (150 g) candied orange peel, 5¼ oz (50 g) candied lemon peel, $^1/_3$ cup + 1 tbsp (50 g) flour, 3 tbsp cocoa powder, 1 tsp ground cinnamon, 1 pinch ground cloves, 1 pinch ground ginger, 1 pinch ground coriander, 1 pinch freshly grated nutmeg, ½ cup (100 g) sugar, $^1/_3$ cup (100 g) honey

To sprinkle on top: parchment paper, ample powdered sugar

Preheat the oven to 390°F (200°C), unless you have a convection oven, in which case preheat to 355°F (180°C), or a gas oven, in which case preheat to level 4. Roast the hazelnuts in the preheated oven for 10 minutes, remove, let cool slightly, and peel by rubbing against each other. Then chop the nuts coarsely.

Reduce the oven temperature to 300°F (15°C). Briefly blanch the almonds in boiling water, and drain in a colander. Allow to cool briefly and then peel. Finely dice the candied orange peel and candied lemon peel. Mix the prepared ingredients with flour, cocoa powder, cinnamon, cloves, ginger, coriander, and nutmeg. Melt sugar and honey in a pot and gently fold into the mixture.

Line a mini springform pan with parchment paper and place one-third of the Panforte dough in it. Place in the preheated oven, and bake for 30 minutes. Take the baking sheet out of the oven and let cool slightly. Remove the Panforte from the pan with a knife, and flip it over onto a countertop covered with powdered sugar. Remove the parchment paper.

Repeat that process with the remaining dough. Before serving, cut the Panforte into wedges and sprinkle with plenty of powdered sugar.

International Specialties

Zaleti (Cornmeal Cookies)

For the dough: ²/₃ cup (100 g) sultanas, ²/₃ cup (150 g) butter or lard, 1¼ cups (150 g) corn-meal, 1 cup + 3 tbsp (150 g) wheat flour (type 00), 2 tsp (8 g) vanilla sugar, 1 pinch salt, 1 tsp (5–6 g) hartshorn salt, 3 eggs, ½ cup (100 g) sugar
Additional: butter for the baking sheet, powdered sugar for sprinkling

Soak the sultanas in warm water for a few minutes and then let them dry on paper towels. Meanwhile, melt the butter or lard in a pot and then let it cool again.

In a bowl, mix the two types of flour, vanilla sugar, salt, and hartshorn salt carefully. In a second bowl, beat the eggs and sugar until fluffy. Add in the flour mixture, cooled fat, and sultanas and knead into a smooth dough. Add a little water or milk if necessary.

Preheat the oven to 355°F (180°C), unless you have a convection oven, in which case preheat to 320°F (160°C), or a gas oven, in which case preheat to level 3. Divide the dough into equal halves and shape each half into a cylindrical roll, 1 in.–1½ in. (3 cm–4 cm) in diameter. Cut the rolls into approximately 2 in. (5 cm) long pieces and then shape into little oval discs (see photo). Place on a greased baking sheet, making sure there is enough distance between each of the cookies. Put the baking sheet in the preheated oven and bake for about 12 minutes, until golden. Then take the cookies out of the oven and let cool on a wire rack. Dust with powdered sugar.

International Specialties

Christmas Fortune Cookies

MAKES 12 FORTUNE COOKIES
For the dough: ¼ cup (35 g) flour, ⅓ cup (35 g) powdered sugar, 1 pinch salt, 2½ tbsp (35 g) butter, 1 egg white
Additional: parchment paper, flour for the baking sheets, 1 teacup (diameter 4 in [10 cm]), butter, spatula, 12 messages of love on thin strips of paper, 1 glass, 1 egg carton

In a mixing bowl, mix flour, powdered sugar, salt, butter, and egg white into a smooth dough. Divide the dough into three parts. Let two of the pieces rest in the refrigerator.

Preheat the oven to 390°F (200°C), unless you have a convection oven, in which case preheat to 355°F (180°C), or a gas oven, in which case preheat to level 4. Line a baking sheet with parchment paper, sprinkle with flour, and roll the third piece of dough out thinly on that surface. Grease the rim of the teacup with butter, and then use it to cut out four circles from the dough. Remove the excess dough from the outside of the circles and combine with the dough that was put away in the refrigerator so you can use it later.

Place the baking sheet in the preheated oven (middle rack) and bake the dough circles for about 5 minutes. Afterward, they should be cooked through, but still very light in color. Take out of the oven and let cool. Then place the baking sheet into the oven again, bake until the dough circles are light brown, and remove from the oven once again.

Remove one dough circle from the baking sheet using a spatula and immediately fold it together, with a message of love inside. Quickly grasp the ends and lay the straight side of the half circle over the edge of a glass and press down, to get the typical fortune cookie shape. Let cool in an egg carton so that the cookies retain their shape. Repeat this process until all the dough and messages of love are used up.

 You should use multiple baking sheets while baking so that they have time to cool before they need to be used again. The baking process must still be interrupted, though, so the dough circles can be evenly browned.

International Specialties

Baking with Children

Cut~Out Cookies & Icing Drizzles

Kneading delicious dough, cutting out the shapes of the Christmas cookies yourself, taking in the scent of the freshly baked treats—these are things that get the whole family into the Christmas spirit. For the classic cookies presented in the following chapter, even the little ones can help.

Cinnamon Stars *

Makes 2 trays

For the dough: 5 egg whites, 3¾ cups (450 g) powdered sugar, 5¼ cups (500 g) ground almonds, 2 tsp ground cinnamon

Additional: sugar for the countertop, cookie cutters, parchment paper, plastic wrap

The cinnamon stars need to sit out overnight before baking. On the preparation day, use a hand mixer with a whisk attachment to beat the egg whites until stiff. Then sift the powdered sugar over the egg whites and fold in gently. Set aside a cup of this egg white mixture to be used as glaze.

In a large bowl, quickly knead the almonds, cinnamon, and 1 tbsp water with the rest of the egg white mixture. Roll the dough into a ball, wrap it in plastic wrap, and place in the refrigerator for 1 hour.

Line the two baking sheets with parchment paper, cut to size. Sprinkle a countertop with sugar and roll out the dough onto it. The dough should be about ²/₅ in. (1 cm) thick.

Use the cookie cutters to cut out stars and snowflakes from the dough, brush them with the egg white mixture (glaze) from the cup, and lay side by side on the lined baking sheets. Then, let the cinnamon stars dry and sit out at room temperature overnight.

The next day, preheat the oven to 320°F (160°C), unless you have a convection oven, in which case preheat to 285°F (140°C), or a gas oven, in which case preheat to level 2. Then, place the cinnamon stars on the baking sheets, on the middle rack, for 7–8 minutes. Afterward, they should still be very light in color and soft on the inside.

Cut-Out Cookies & Icing Drizzles

Vanilla Cookies *

MAKES 2 TRAYS

For the dough: 2¼ cups (280 g) flour, ½ cup (50 g) ground almonds, ½ cup (50 g) ground hazelnuts, ¹/₃ cup (70 g) sugar, 1 tbsp (12 g) bourbon vanilla sugar, 1 pinch salt, ¾ cup + 3 tbsp (210 g) cold butter
Additional: cookie press, parchment paper, plastic wrap

Place the flour, almonds, nuts, sugar, vanilla sugar, and salt on a countertop. Cut butter into small pieces and distribute on top of the other ingredients. Mix everything together, first with your fingertips and then by kneading into a smooth dough.

Shape the dough into an approximately 2 in. (5 cm) thick, cylindrical roll, wrap in plastic wrap, and place in the refrigerator for 2 hours.

Preheat the oven to 355°F (180°C), unless you have a convection oven, in which case preheat to 320°F (160°C), or a gas oven, in which case preheat to level 3. Line two baking sheets with parchment paper, cut to size. Select an attachment (i.e. a flower or a star) for the cookie press and attach it to the appliance. Put the dough into the cookie press, a little at a time, and use the machine to place the cookies directly on the lined baking sheets.

Place the baking sheets into the preheated oven on the middle rack. Bake for 8–10 minutes.

Take the cookies out of the oven when they have just barely changed color, but are still quite light. Allow the cookies to cool slightly and then remove them from the baking sheets with a spatula. Carefully set them next to each other on a wire rack and let them cool further.

Cut-Out Cookies & Icing Drizzles

Chocolate Stripes

MAKES 2 TRAYS

For the dough: 3½ oz (100 g) good-quality dark couverture chocolate, ¾ cup + 2 tbsp (200 g) butter, ½ cup + ¹/₃ cup (100 g) powdered sugar, 1 pinch salt, 2 egg yolks, ¾ cup + 2 tsp (80 g) ground hazelnuts, zest from 2 organic oranges, 2¹/₃ cup + 1 tbsp (300 g) spelt or wheat flour, 5¼ oz (150 g) good-quality dark chocolate glaze
Additional: parchment paper, piping bag with a star tip or mincer with a star attachment

Chop the couverture into chunks and place into a bowl. Place a pot of warm water on the stove, place the bowl inside, and let the couverture melt slowly over low heat. Caution: Do not get any water in the bowl.

Place the butter into a mixing bowl and, using a hand mixer with the whisk attachment, beat for 5–10 minutes, until foamy. Gradually add in powdered sugar, salt, egg yolks, nuts, melted couverture, orange zest, and flour.

Preheat the oven to 355°F (180°C), unless you have a convection oven, in which case preheat to 320°F (160°C), or a gas oven, in which case preheat to level 3. Line both baking sheets with parchment paper, cut to size.

Place the dough into a piping bag with a star tip or in a mincer with a star attachment. Using one of those appliances, make approximately 4 in. (10 cm) long strips of dough and place them onto the baking sheets.

Place the baking sheets on the middle rack of the preheated oven and bake the stripes for 8–10 minutes.

Take the baking sheets out of the oven and let cool for 5 minutes. Then, using a spatula, place the cookies onto a wire rack to cool.

Melt the chocolate glaze according to the package directions and dip half of each cookie in it. Place on the wire rack again and let dry.

Cut-Out Cookies & Icing Drizzles

Flower-Shaped Butter Biscuits with Hagelzucker *

MAKES 2 TRAYS

For the dough: ²/₃ cup (150 g) butter, ½ cup (100 g) sugar, 1 pinch salt, a little bit of zest from an organic orange, 1 egg, 2 cups (250 g) flour
To knead in: flour, ¼ cup (50 g) coarse sugar
Additional: rosette cookie cutters, parchment paper, plastic wrap

Mix butter and sugar with salt and orange zest in a mixing bowl. Gently crack an egg, let the egg white slide into a small bowl, and set aside. Add the egg yolk to the rest of the ingredients. Sift in the flour and knead everything into a smooth dough. Then roll the dough into a ball, wrap it in plastic wrap, and let it sit in the refrigerator for 2 hours.

Preheat the oven to 390°F (200°C), unless you have a convection oven, in which case preheat to 355°F (180°C), or a gas oven, in which case preheat to level 4. Line two baking sheets with parchment paper, cut to size.

Roll out the dough on a floured surface until it is approximately ¹/₁₀ in. (3 mm) thick and cut into cookies using a rosette cookie cutter. Then make a hole in the center of each dough flower, using a small round cookie cutter.

For decoration, whisk the egg white in a glass with a fork, brush the rosettes with it, sprinkle with coarse sugar, and press down on the sugar crystals lightly.

Place the cookies next to each other on the lined baking sheets. Place the baking sheets on the middle rack of the preheated oven and bake for 12–15 minutes, until the dough rings are light brown.

Allow each baking sheet to cool for 5 minutes after it has been removed from the oven. Only then should the cookies be removed from the baking sheets with a spatula and placed onto a wire rack to cool.

130

Cut-Out Cookies & Icing Drizzles

Butter Cookies with a Message **

MAKES 2 TRAYS

For the dough: ²/₃ cup (150 g) butter, ¹/₃ cup + 4 tsp (50 g) powdered sugar, 1 tsp vanilla sugar, 1 pinch salt, ¼ cup (50 g) sour cream, 2 cups + 3 tbsp (275 g) flour

Additional: flour to knead in, parchment paper, cookie cutters (e.g., rocking horse, tractor, train, or car), 1 alphabet stamp set (available for purchase at a household specialty store or on the Internet), plastic wrap

Mix butter, powdered sugar, vanilla sugar, and salt in a bowl. Gradually add flour and sour cream and knead everything into a smooth dough. Roll the dough into a ball, wrap in plastic wrap, and let rest for 1 hour in the refrigerator.

Preheat the oven to 375°F (190°C), unless you have a convection oven, in which case preheat to 340°F (170°C), or a gas oven, in which case preheat to level 3–4. Line two baking sheets with parchment paper, cut to size. Prepare the alphabet embossing set to stamp a name, or a message of your choice, such as ANGELS or MERRY CHRISTMAS.

Roll out the dough on a floured surface until it is ¹/₁₀ in. (3 mm) thick, cut out different shapes with the cookie cutters, and stamp the prepared words into the cookies.

Place the cookies next to each other on the lined baking sheets. Then place the baking sheets one after another into the preheated oven (middle rack) and bake the butter cookies for 8–10 minutes until very lightly colored.

Allow each baking sheet to cool for 5 minutes after it has been removed from the oven. Only then should the biscuits be removed from the baking sheets with a spatula and placed onto a wire rack to cool.

Cut-Out Cookies & Icing Drizzles

Colorful Frosted Cookies ✴✴

MAKES 2 TRAYS

For the dough: 3 cups (380 g) flour, 1 pinch salt, 1 cup (120 g) powdered sugar, 1 cup +
1½ tbsp (250 g) cold butter, 2 eggs
For decorating: 8¾ oz (250 g) assorted red and yellow jams, powdered sugar for sprinkling
Additional: assorted cookie cutters (e.g., circles with wavy edges, flowers, stars), plastic wrap

Mix flour, salt, and powdered sugar on a countertop. Cut the butter into small pieces, place
them on top of the flour mixture, and rub the ingredients together with the tip of your
fingers until crumbly.

Carefully crack the eggs one at a time. Let the egg white slide into a small bowl and set
aside. Add the egg yolk to the remaining ingredients and knead into a smooth dough. Roll
the dough into a ball, wrap in plastic wrap, and let sit in the refrigerator for 30 minutes.

Preheat the oven to 355°F (180°C), unless you have a convection oven, in which case
preheat to 320°F (160°C), or a gas oven, in which case preheat to level 3. Line two baking
sheets with parchment paper, cut to size.

Separate the dough into pieces, roll out to a thickness of $^1/_{10}$ in. (3 mm), and cut out an
even number of cookies, half with a hole in the middle, half without. Put the cookies next
to each other on the baking sheets. Then place the baking sheets on the middle rack of the
preheated oven, and bake for 8–10 minutes, until the cookies are very lightly colored.

Meanwhile, heat up both the yellow and the red jams separately, each in a small pot with
1–2 tbsp water.

Allow each baking sheet to cool for 5 minutes after it has been removed from the oven.
Only then should the cookies be removed from the baking sheets with a spatula and placed
onto a wire rack to cool. Place ¼ teaspoon of jam on the center of a cookie without a hole
and put an identically shaped cookie, with a hole in it, on top. Repeat this process until all
of the cookies have been stuck together. Lastly, dust the cookies with powdered sugar.

Cut-Out Cookies & Icing Drizzles

Spritz Rings **

MAKES 2 TRAYS

For the dough: 2⅓ cup + 1 tbsp (300 g) spelt or wheat flour, 1 cup + 2½ tbsp (140 g) powdered sugar, 2 tsp (8 g) bourbon vanilla sugar, 1 pinch salt, 1 cup (100 g) ground almonds (blanched), 1 cup (240 g) butter, 1 egg yolk
Additional: piping bag with a star tip or mincer with star attachment, plastic wrap

Sift the flour onto a countertop. Add powdered sugar, vanilla sugar, salt, almonds, butter cut into small pieces, and egg yolk to the flour, and knead all of the ingredients together into a smooth dough.

Roll the dough into a ball, wrap in plastic wrap, and let rest for at least 1 hour in the refrigerator.

Preheat the oven to 355°F (180°C), unless you have a convection oven, in which case preheat to 320°F (160°C), or a gas oven, in which case preheat to level 3. Line two baking sheets with parchment paper, cut to size.

Place the dough into a piping bag with a star tip or into a mincer with a star attachment. Using one of those tools, make approximately 3–3½ in. (7–9 cm) dough rings, squeezing them directly onto the lined baking sheets. Either press the ends of the rings together or lay one end over another to form a cross shape and press down gently.

Place the baking sheets on the middle rack of the preheated oven and bake the rings for about 10 minutes, until they are lightly colored.

Allow each baking sheet to cool for 5 minutes after it has been removed from the oven. Only then should the spritz rings be removed from the baking sheets with a spatula and placed onto a wire rack to cool.

Cut-Out Cookies & Icing Drizzles

Nut Bars for Kids

MAKES 1 SMALL TRAY

For the dough: 1 cup + 1½ tbsp (250 g) soft butter, 3½ oz (100 g) sugar beet syrup, 3½ oz (100 g) raw cane sugar, 2 tsp (8 g) vanilla sugar, 2 eggs, 7 oz (200 g) raisins, 2½ cups (400 g) crisp oats, 3 tsp baking powder, 1 cup (100 g) ground hazelnuts, ½ cup + 1 tbsp (100 g) chopped hazelnuts

For the glaze: 9 oz (250 g) good-quality dark chocolate glaze

Additional: parchment paper

Preheat the oven to 355°F (180°C), unless you have a convection oven, in which case preheat to 320°F (160°C), or a gas oven, in which case preheat to level 3. Line a baking sheet with parchment paper, cut to size.

Place the butter in a mixing bowl and, using a hand mixer with a whisk attachment, beat 5–10 minutes, until foamy. Add in the sugar beet syrup, sugar, and vanilla sugar, and stir until the sugar crystals have dissolved.

Add in eggs and raisins. Mix the oatmeal and baking powder together and fold into the mixture 1 tbsp at a time. Finally, mix in the ground and chopped hazelnuts.

Spread the nut mixture onto the baking sheet evenly, approximately ²/₅ in. (1 cm) thick. Place the baking sheet on the middle rack of the preheated oven and bake the nut bars for about 30 minutes, until they are golden brown.

Then take the baking sheet carefully out of the oven and let the sheet of nut bars cool completely.

Melt the chocolate glaze according to the directions on the package.

Cut the nut bars into any shape you desire, dip two edges or corners of each shape in the chocolate glaze, and place side by side on a wire rack or parchment paper to dry.

Cut-Out Cookies & Icing Drizzles

Shaping and Building

Whether you are rolling truffles or building a gingerbread house like a master builder, everyone will find their personal challenge in the following recipes. The younger ones can also demonstrate their skills, especially when making oatmeal cookies and chocolate cornflake clusters.

Advent Waffles*

MAKES 6 WAFFLES

For the dough: 1 cup + 1½ tbsp (250 g) butter, 1 cup (200 g) sugar, 1 tsp (4 g) bourbon vanilla sugar, 1 pinch salt, 2¹⁄₃ cup + 1 tbsp (300 g) flour, 1 tsp baking powder, 1 tsp ground cinnamon, 6 eggs

Additional: waffle iron, powdered sugar to sprinkle on top

Use a hand mixer with a whisk attachment to beat butter, sugar, vanilla sugar, and salt in a mixing bowl until creamy. In another bowl, mix flour, baking powder, and cinnamon together. Next, alternate adding in approximately 3 tbsp of the flour mixture and 1 egg to the buttercream, while mixing everything together into a smooth dough.

Heat up the waffle iron. Pour a small ladle of batter in and bake until a golden brown waffle has formed. Repeat this process to make more waffles.

With a fork, remove the waffles from the waffle iron and pile on a plate. Directly before serving, sprinkle the waffles with powdered sugar. They taste their very best when they are fresh.

 On hot waffles, whipped cream thickened with a little bit of cornstarch tastes wonderful!

Shaping and Building

 Oatmeal Cookies *

For the dough: ¹/₃ cup + 2 tbsp (100 g) butter, ¼ cup (50 g) granulated brown sugar, ¼ cup (50 g) white sugar, 1 tsp (4 g) bourbon vanilla sugar, ¾ cup + 1¼ tbsp (100 g) wheat-whole grain flour, 1 tsp baking powder, 1 pinch salt, 1 egg, 1 tbsp milk, ½ cup (80 g) oats, ¼ cup + ½ tbsp (50 g) coarsely chopped hazelnuts, 3½–5 oz (100–150 g) finely chopped assorted dried fruit

Additional: parchment paper

Beat the butter, both types of sugar, and vanilla sugar in a bowl until fluffy.

In a second bowl, mix the flour with baking powder and salt, add in the egg and milk, and mix everything into the butter-sugar mixture. Then knead in the oats, nuts, and dried fruit. Cover the dough in the bowl with a cloth and place the bowl in the refrigerator for 1 hour.

Preheat the oven to 355°F (180°C), unless you have a convection oven, in which case preheat to 320°F (160°C), or a gas oven, in which case preheat to level 3. Line two baking sheets with parchment paper, cut to size.

Place 1 heaping tsp of dough on the lined baking sheet for each cookie. Make sure you leave enough distance between the cookies, as the dough tends to spread out a bit during baking.

Place the baking sheets on the middle rack of the preheated oven and bake the cookies for 12–15 minutes, until they are golden brown.

Allow each baking sheet to cool for 5 minutes after it has been removed from the oven. Only then should the oatmeal cookies be removed from the baking sheets with a spatula and placed onto a wire rack to cool. In a tin can, they will stay very fresh.

Shaping and Building

Chocolate Cornflake Clusters *

Makes 1 tray

For the clusters: 7 oz (200 g) good-quality dark couverture chocolate, 2¾ oz (80 g) whole grain cornflakes

Additional: parchment paper

Line a baking sheet with parchment paper, cut to size.

Cut half of the couverture into chunks and place it into a small bowl. Place a pot of warm water on the stove, place the small bowl inside it, and let the couverture melt slowly over low heat. Caution: there must be no water in the small bowl.

Meanwhile, finely chop the second half of the couverture with a knife and as soon as the warm couverture is melted, mix in the chocolate shavings. This creates a thick chocolate sauce.

Mix the whole grain cornflakes in with the chocolate sauce and use 2 tsp to place the clusters onto the baking sheet. Leave some space between each cluster so they do not run into each other.

Finally, set aside the chocolate cornflake clusters and let them harden. In a tin can, they will stay very fresh.

Shaping and Building

Coconut Truffles *

MAKES 1 SMALL TRAY

For the confectionery: 8¾ oz (250 g) white couverture chocolate, ½ cup + 1½ tsp (¹/₈ l) cream, 2 oz (60 g) coconut oil, 7 oz (200 g) coconut flakes to roll in
Additional: parchment paper, piping bag with a round tip, approximately 30 small paper liners

Chop the couverture into small pieces with a knife. Place the cream and coconut oil in a pot and bring to a boil. As soon as the mixture boils, remove it from heat.

Add in the chopped couverture and stir until it has melted. Let cool a bit at room temperature and then place in the refrigerator to let cool completely. This takes about 1 hour.

Line a small baking sheet with parchment paper, cut to size. Pour the chocolate mixture into a piping bag with a round tip and squeeze bonbon-sized discs onto the baking sheet, making sure to leave enough distance between them. Then chill in the refrigerator once more for 1 hour.

Pour the coconut flakes onto a flat plate. Take the chocolate discs from the refrigerator and use cool hands to roll them into balls. Then roll the balls in the coconut flakes and place them into the paper liners.

Shaping and Building

Easy Truffles with Chocolate Sprinkles *

MAKES 1 TRAY
For the truffles: 15¾ oz (450 g) dark couverture chocolate, 1¼ cups (300 ml) cream
For the couverture: chocolate sprinkles
Additional: parchment paper, piping bag with a round tip, approximately 30 colorful tin mini-muffin cups

Chop the chocolate into chunks with a knife.

Put the cream in a pot, bring it to a boil, and then remove from heat. Add in the couverture and let it melt in the cream as you stir.

Take the pot off the heat and let the chocolate mixture cool. Then leave in the refrigerator to harden for about 1 hour.

Line a baking sheet with parchment paper, cut to size. Pour the chocolate cream into a piping bag with a round tip and squeeze chocolate discs onto the baking sheet, making sure to leave enough space between them. Let cool in the refrigerator again for 1 hour.

Meanwhile, fill a shallow baking pan or a deep plate with chocolate sprinkles. Take the chocolate discs out of the refrigerator and roll with cool hands into balls. Then roll the balls in the chocolate sprinkles and place into the mini-muffin cups. When packaged in this way, the truffles can be a particularly nice gift.

Shaping and Building

Black and White Snails ✱✱

MAKES 2 TRAYS

For the dough: 3 cups + 2 tsp (380 g) flour, 1 cup (120 g) powdered sugar, 1 pinch salt,
1 cup + 1½ tbsp (250 g) cold butter, 2 eggs, 1 heaping tsp cocoa powder
Additional: a little bit of flour to knead in, parchment paper, plastic wrap

Mix the flour, powdered sugar, and salt on a countertop. Place little pieces of butter on top
and incorporate into the flour mixture to form a crumbly dough.

Crack the eggs carefully, one at a time, and let the egg whites slide into a small bowl
(they can be used elsewhere). Add the egg yolks to the remaining ingredients and knead
everything quickly into a smooth dough.

Divide the dough into two equal halves and knead cocoa powder into one half. Form
two balls, one dark and one light, wrap them both in plastic wrap, and let stand for 2 hours
in the refrigerator.

Preheat the oven to 355°F (180°C), unless you have a convection oven, in which case
preheat to 320°F (160°C), or a gas oven, in which case preheat to level 3. Line two baking
sheets with parchment paper, cut to size.

Form walnut-sized balls from both the light and the dark dough and roll them out into
6–8 in. (15–20 cm) long cylindrical rolls, all with the same, consistent thickness. Press the
light and the dark rolls of dough together slightly and roll up like a snail (see photo). Place
the snails on the lined baking sheet.

Put the baking sheets one after another on the middle rack of the preheated oven and bake
each batch of snails for 12 minutes, until they are lightly colored.

Allow each baking sheet to cool for 5 minutes after it has been removed from the oven.
Only then should the cookies be removed from the baking sheets with a spatula and placed
onto a wire rack to cool.

Shaping and Building

Bread Men and Women **

MAKES 1 TRAY

For the dough: 5¼ oz (150 g) low-fat quark, 6 tbsp milk, 6 tbsp neutral cooking oil, ⅓ cup + 2 tsp (75 g) sugar, 2 tsp (8 g) vanilla sugar, 1 pinch salt, 2⅓ cup + 1 tbsp (300 g) flour, 1 tbsp (10 g) baking powder
For garnishing: raisins
Additional: parchment paper, egg yolk to brush onto the dough

Remove excess liquid from the low-fat quark using a paper towel. Then, mix the quark, milk, oil, sugar, vanilla sugar, and salt in a bowl. Sift the flour into a second bowl and mix with baking soda. Add half of the flour mixture, 1 tbsp at a time, to the quark mixture, and mix it in. Then knead in the rest of the flour mixture with your hands.

Preheat the oven to 355°F (180°C), unless you have a convection oven, in which case preheat to 320°F (160°C), or a gas oven, in which case preheat to level 3. Line a baking sheet with parchment paper, cut to size.

Out of the dough, make balls for the heads, long cylinders for the arms and legs, as well as a body and garments for the bread men and women. They should be about 8 in. (20 cm) tall. For the eyes and the mouths, press raisins into the faces of the dough people. Brush the bread men and women with beaten egg yolk.

Place the bread men and women onto a baking sheet, making sure to leave enough space for the bread to expand a little bit. Put the baking sheet on the middle rack of the preheated oven and bake for 30 minutes, until golden brown.

Allow the baking sheet to cool for 5–10 minutes after it has been removed from the oven. Only then should the bread be removed from the baking sheets with a spatula and placed onto a wire rack to cool. This bread is best enjoyed not long after baking.

Shaping and Building

Gingerbread Men and Women ✳✳

MAKES 2 TRAYS

For the dough: ¹/₃ cup + 2 tbsp (100 g) butter, ¾ cup (250 g) honey, ½ cup + 2 tbsp (125 g) sugar, ¼ oz (7½ g) gingerbread spice, 1 tbsp cocoa powder, 4¾ cup + 2 tsp (600 g) flour, 1 tsp (4 g) baking powder, 1 pinch salt, 1 egg
For the garnish: 2 egg whites, 3 cups + 2 tbsp (375 g) powdered sugar, bright mini sugar pearls
Additional: flour for the countertop, cookie cutters for gingerbread men and women, grease-proof paper, aluminum foil

The gingerbread dough must sit out for a night before baking, so on the day of preparation, place the butter, with honey, sugar, gingerbread spice, and cocoa powder, in a pot. Warm over low heat, stirring constantly, and wait for the sugar to completely dissolve. Then take the pan off the heat and allow the honey mixture to cool.

Sift the flour and baking powder into a bowl, add in the honey mixture, salt and egg, and knead everything into a smooth dough. Shape the dough into a ball, wrap in aluminum foil, turn a bowl upside-down over it, and let stand overnight at room temperature.

The next day, preheat the oven to 390°F (200°C), unless you have a convection oven, in which case preheat to 355°F (180°C), or a gas oven, in which case preheat to level 4. Line two baking sheets with parchment paper, cut to size.

Roll out the dough on a floured surface until it is approximately ¹/₅ in. (½ cm) thick, cut out the gingerbread men and women, and lay them out on the baking sheets, making sure to leave enough space for the bread to expand a little bit. Put the baking sheets in the pre-heated oven, on the middle rack, for 12–15 minutes. After taking each baking sheet out of the oven, immediately lift the gingerbread people off the tray with a spatula, and place on a wire rack to cool.

For the decoration, using a hand mixer with a whisk attachment, beat the egg whites with enough sifted powdered sugar that a fairly solid mass forms. Out of half of a sheet of parchment paper, make a piping bag, fill it with the icing, and cut a small hole at the end. Finally, decorate the gingerbread men as desired with the icing and colored sprinkles.

Shaping and Building

Mini Cookie Houses  ✸✸✸

MAKES 1 TRAY

For the houses: 12 rectangular shortbread biscuits (approximately 2$^1/_3$ in. x 2 in. [6 cm x 5 cm], ready-made product)

For the garnish: 4 egg whites, 1 pinch salt, ½ cup + 2 tbsp (125 g) sugar, ½ cup + $^1/_3$ cup (100 g) powdered sugar, ½ oz (15 g) starch, 10½ oz (300 g) marshmallows, a few mini-marshmallows, miniature rectangular chocolate cookies, bright mini sugar pearls

Additional: parchment paper, wax paper

The gingerbread houses need one night to dry. On the day of preparation, use a hand mixer with a whisk attachment to beat the egg whites and salt in a bowl until creamy, while gradually sprinkling in sugar. Keep mixing until the crystals have dissolved. This mixture will be used as the snow decoration. In another bowl, mix powdered sugar and starch, sift it over the egg white mixture, and fold in gently.

Make a piping bag out of parchment paper, fill it with the glaze, and cut a small hole in the tip. Use the icing to glue 2 marshmallows on top of each other, and the marshmallows onto the middle of 4 cookies. Cover the top of the higher marshmallows with the egg white mixture.

Glue 2 cookies together on the long sides using the egg white mixture to form a pointed roof. Glue this onto the top marshmallow. Hold the roof together with your hands until the house can stand on its own. Use this process to build three more mini cookie houses.

Line a baking sheet with parchment paper, cut to size, place the cookie houses on it, and let dry overnight at room temperature. Cover the rest of the egg white mixture and place in the refrigerator.

The next day, make a second piping bag out of half a sheet of wax paper, fill it with the egg white mixture, and cut a small hole in the top of the bag.

Decorate the house roofs with snow (the egg white mixture), mini chocolate cookies, sugar pearls, etc. Make fences out of mini-marshmallows or fruit gummies (see photo). Finally, use the egg white mixture to stick a small, rectangular cookie on the roof as a chimney.

Shaping and Building

Gingerbread House ✪✪✪

MAKES 2 TRAYS

For the dough: double the amount of the ingredients used for the gingerbread men and women (see page 154)

For the garnish: 4 egg whites, 1 pinch salt, ½ cup + 2 tbsp (125 g) sugar, ½ cup + ⅓ cup (100 g) powdered sugar, ½ oz (15 g) starch, colorful nonpareils, mini chocolate cookies, M&M's, Mini M&M's, red-and-white peppermint candies, mini marshmallows, etc.

Additional: gingerbread house cookie cutters (specialty shop or Internet)

Prepare the gingerbread dough the day before baking, as described on page 154, and let it rest overnight at room temperature under a bowl.

The following day, preheat the oven to 390°F (200°C), unless you have a convection oven, in which case preheat to 355°F (180°C), or a gas oven, in which case preheat to level 4. Line two baking sheets with parchment paper, cut to size. Roll out the dough on a floured countertop, until it is about ⅛ in. (4 mm) thick. With the gingerbread house cookie cutters, cut out 2 gables and 2 rectangular house walls. Cut out windows and a door with a pastry wheel or knife. For the roof, roll out the dough thinner, and with rectangular gingerbread house cookie cutters, cut out four panels. Use the remaining pastry to roll out a 8 in. x 12 in. (20 cm x 30 cm) sheet and use it as a foundation.

Place all parts next to each other on the baking sheets and bake the gingerbread for 12–15 minutes in the oven. Take the trays out of the oven and, while the gingerbread is still hot, remove it from the baking sheet using a spatula and place it onto a wire rack to cool.

For decoration, beat the egg whites and salt with the hand mixer until creamy. Sprinkle in the sugar slowly and continue to beat the mixture until the sugar has dissolved. Sieve powdered sugar and starch into a second bowl and fold the mixture into the egg whites carefully. Pour the egg white mixture into a piping bag with a round tip. With that mixture, glue 2 roof panels together on the long sides and allow to dry for about 1 hour. Next, use the egg white mixture to glue the 2 gables and 2 house walls onto the foundation at right angles. Support with glasses and let dry for about 1–2 hours. Glue both sides of the roof onto the gable with the egg white mixture. Now decorate the gingerbread house with the egg white mixture and colorful candy to your liking (see photo).

Baking and Decorating Cakes

While decorating a Christmas cake, the little ones can let their imaginations run wild and be creative with icing, glaze, and bright sugar pearls. Or they can simply sprinkle baked goods with a bit of powdered sugar. Those end up looking beautiful, as if snow has just fallen upon them.

Mini Christmas Bundt Cakes *

MAKES 6 MINIATURE BUNDT CAKES

For the dough: $^1/_3$ cup (70 ml) lukewarm milk, ¾ oz (20 g) yeast, 1½ cups + 5 tsp (200 g) flour, 2 eggs, $^1/_3$ cup + 2 tbsp (100 g) butter, ¼ cup + 2½ tsp (60 g) sugar, 1 pinch salt, zest from ½ organic lemon, 2½ oz (75 g) chocolate chips and/or raisins

Additional: a little bit of soft butter for the pan, breadcrumbs for the pan, wooden skewers, powdered sugar for sprinkling

For the pre-ferment, put milk into a bowl, crumble in the yeast, dissolve it, and fold in 1 tbsp of flour. Now cover the pre-ferment with a kitchen towel, and let sit in a warm, draft-free place until it has doubled in size.

Place the leftover flour in a mixing bowl and make a deep trough in the middle. Carefully crack open an egg and separate the egg white from the yolk. Place the egg yolk, another egg, pre-ferment, butter, sugar, salt, and lemon peel into the flour trough and knead thoroughly into a sticky dough. Place this dough in a bowl and cover it with a kitchen towel. Let it rise in a warm, draft-free place until it has doubled in size. Then knead in the chocolate chips and/or raisins.

Preheat the oven to 355°F (180°C), unless you have a convection oven, in which case preheat to 320°F (160°C), or a gas oven, in which case preheat to level 3. Butter the molds of the mini Bundt pan, sprinkle in the breadcrumbs, and shake out those that don't stick. Evenly distribute the dough amongst the molds.

Place the pan on the middle rack of the preheated oven and bake the mini Bundt cakes for 35–40 minutes. Stick a toothpick into the middle of a little cake. If the dough doesn't stick to it, take the pan carefully out of the oven. Otherwise let the cakes bake for another 5 minutes. After taking the mini Bundt cakes out of the oven, let them sit for 5 minutes, turn them upside-down onto a cooling rack, and let them cool completely. As a final touch, sprinkle with powdered sugar.

Baking and Decorating Cakes

Christmas Cake in a Jar **

Makes 7 jars containing 6¾ ounces (200 ml)

For the dough: 5¼ oz (150 g) dark couverture chocolate, 1 large can pears, ½ cup + 1 tbsp (125 g) butter, ⅔ cup (130 g) sugar, 2 tsp (8 g) vanilla sugar, 1 pinch salt, 4 eggs, 1⅓ cup + 2 tbsp (180 g) flour, 1 tbsp cocoa powder, 1¾ oz (50 g) ground almonds, 2 tbsp powdered sugar

For the trees: wrapping paper, 7 wooden skewers, 7 mini marshmallows

Additional: soft butter and flour for the jars, powdered sugar for sprinkling

Coarsely chop the couverture and place into a bowl. Heat up a pot of warm water on the stove and place the bowl into the pot so the couverture can melt slowly over low heat. Caution: water must not get into the bowl. Lift the bowl out of the water bath as soon as the couverture has melted.

Preheat the oven to 355°F (180°C), unless you have a convection oven, in which case preheat to 320°F (160°C), or a gas oven, in which case preheat to level 3. Thoroughly butter and flour the jars. Remove excess flour from the jars by shaking them. Drain the pears in a sieve, catch the pear juice in a bowl, and coarsely chop the fruit.

Using a hand mixer with a whisk attachment, beat butter, sugar, vanilla sugar, and salt in a bowl until creamy. Add in the cooled couverture and keep stirring for several minutes.

Crack the eggs one after another, separate the egg whites from the yolks, and mix the yolk in with the dough. In a separate bowl, mix flour, cocoa powder, and almonds and stir that mixture into the dough. Beat the egg whites with powdered sugar until stiff peaks form. Then carefully fold the egg white mixture into the dough.

Next, distribute the dough amongst the jars and bake them on the middle rack of the pre-heated oven for 35–40 minutes. Afterward, place the cake on a wire rack and let cool.

♥ Using a cookie cutter as a stencil, trace fourteen Christmas trees on a piece of gift wrap and cut them out. Glue them together with a skewer in between, inscribe with a name, and stick mini-marshmallows on the treetops. Place every jar in a paper muffin liner, sprinkle with powdered sugar, and stick the paper Christmas trees into the jars. These make for great table decorations.

Mini Muffin Advent Calendar**

MAKES 1 TRAY OF 24 MINI MUFFINS

For the dough: 2 eggs, ½ cup + 1 tbsp (125 g) butter, ½ cup + 2 tbsp (125 g) sugar, 1 tsp (4 g) vanilla sugar, 1 pinch salt, 1 cup + 3 tbsp (150 g) flour, ½ tbsp (5 g) baking powder, 2–3 tbsp milk, 1 oz (30 g) ground almonds
For the frosting: 1 egg white, 1 cup (120 g) powdered sugar
For decorating: bright-colored icing in a tube, colorful mini sugar pearls
Additional: 24 mini paper muffin liners

Preheat oven to 355°F (180°C), unless you have a convection oven, in which case preheat to 320°F (160°C), or a gas oven, in which case preheat to level 2. Place the muffin liners in the muffin pan.

Carefully crack 2 eggs, one after another, and separate the egg whites from the yolk. In a mixing bowl, beat butter, $^1/_3$ cup (60 g) sugar, vanilla sugar, and salt into a light cream. Slowly fold in the egg yolks. In a second bowl, mix the flour with the baking powder and gently stir in the milk. Using a hand mixer with the whisk attachment, beat the egg whites and the rest of the sugar until stiff peaks form. Slowly fold in the ground almonds. Then fold the almond-egg white mixture into the dough. Next, distribute the dough with a spoon into the paper liners in the muffin pans.

Place the muffin pan on the middle rack of the preheated oven and let bake for 20–25 minutes. Then take it out of the oven and let cool for several minutes. Lift the muffins along with the muffin liners out of the pan and let cool further on a cooling rack.

For the frosting, lightly beat the egg whites with a fork, sift in powdered sugar, and mix together. Carefully add 2 tbsp of water until the frosting is a spreadable mass. Coat the mini muffins with the frosting, number them 1–24 using colored tube icing, and while the frosting is still soft, decorate with sugar pearls.

♥ If desired, you can put a special emphasis on muffin no. 24 by using a dark chocolate glaze.

Baking and Decorating Cakes

Christmas Star Cake **

Makes 1 star-shaped cake (from a star-shaped cake pan that holds approximately 40 fluid oz [1.2 liters])

For the dough: 1 cup (230 g) butter, 1 cup + 2½ tbsp (230 g) sugar, 1 tsp (8 g) bourbon vanilla sugar, 1 pinch salt, 4 eggs, 2 cups (200 g) ground hazelnuts, 2 cups + 3 tbsp (270 g) flour, (70 g) starch, 1 package baking powder, 2¾ oz (75 g) chocolate chips
For the glaze: 8¾ oz (250 g) good-quality dark chocolate glaze
Additional: butter and flour for the pan, wooden skewers

Note: If you would like to approximate German baking powder you can mix readily-available cream of tartar with baking soda in a 2:1 ratio.

Preheat oven to 355°F (180°C), unless you have a convection oven, in which case preheat to 320°F (160°C), or a gas oven, in which case preheat to level 3. Butter and flour the star-shaped cake pan.

Mix butter, ½ cup + 1 tbsp (115 g) sugar, vanilla sugar, and salt in a bowl and beat until creamy, using a hand mixer. Crack the eggs one after another and separate the egg whites from the yolks. Collect the egg whites in a small bowl and slowly mix the yolk in with the other ingredients in the mixing bowl. Add the other ½ cup + 1 tbsp (115 g) sugar to the egg whites and beat until stiff.

In a third mixing bowl, mix together nuts, flour, starch, and baking powder, and then stir that mixture into the dough. Carefully fold in the beaten egg yolks and chocolate chips. While doing that, stir as little as possible! Then fill the cake pan with dough, making sure to spread it out as evenly as possible.

Place the cake on the middle rack of the preheated oven and bake for about 60 minutes. Poke a hole in the middle of the cake with a toothpick. If the dough sticks to it, bake for another 5 minutes. If not, the cake can be taken out carefully. Let the cake rest in the pan for about 10 minutes. Then flip it over onto a cooling rack and let cool fully.

Melt the chocolate glaze according to the instructions on the package, pour it evenly over the cake, and let harden in a cool place.

♥ If desired, you can decorate the cake with four red Christmas tree candles to celebrate the season.

Christmas Pie ✹✹✹

Makes 1 pie or quiche pan (diameter 9½ in [24 cm])

For the dough: 2 cups (250 g) flour, ½ tsp baking powder, ½ cup (100 g) sugar, 1 pinch salt, ½ cup (50 g) ground hazelnuts, 1 tsp ground cinnamon, ½ cup + 1 tbsp (130 g) cold butter, 1 egg

For the filling: 1 package frozen mixed berries (14 oz /400 g), 4¼ oz (120 g) preserving sugar, 1 tbsp starch

Additional: a little bit of soft butter and breadcrumbs for the pan, flour for the countertop, star-shaped cookie cutters, powdered sugar for sprinkling, plastic wrap

For the filling, leave the mixed berries out at room temperature to thaw. In the meantime, butter the pan and coat it with breadcrumbs. Carefully shake out the crumbs that don't stick.

For the dough, mix flour, baking powder, sugar, salt, nuts, and cinnamon in a bowl. Cut cold butter into pieces and add it to the mixture along with the egg. Using your fingertips, rub everything together until crumbly and then knead into a smooth dough. Roll the dough into a ball, wrap it in plastic wrap, and let rest in the refrigerator for 30 minutes.

Preheat the oven to 355°F (180°C), unless you have a convection oven, in which case preheat to 320°F (160°C), or a gas oven, in which case preheat to level 3. Divide the dough into two pieces, one slightly bigger that the other. Roll out the bigger piece into a circle on a floured surface. The circle should be a little bit bigger than the pan. Line the pan with the dough, pulling the dough up at on the sides, so that it stretches over the edges. Thoroughly mix preserving sugar and starch into the thawed berries and spread onto the pie crust. Fold the excess dough inward over the filling.

On a floured surface, roll the second half of the dough into a circle with a diameter of 9½ in. (24 cm). This will be the top crust of the pie. Use the cookie cutters to cut stars out of the top crust and put the stars aside. Place the top crust onto the pie and press down on the rim, squeezing the two crusts together using your fingertips. Place the star-shaped pieces of dough on top of the pie in between the star-shaped openings.

Bake the pie on the middle rack of the preheated oven for 45–50 minutes, until golden brown. Carefully remove from the oven, place onto a wire rack, and let cool.

♥ Before serving sprinkle with powdered sugar.

Baking and Decorating Cakes

Index

International Specialties